Regarding *Curse of Interesting Times*

Pat Paul's début memoir *Curse of Interesting Times* hits any Baby-Boomer between the eyes with the jarring truths of the late '60s and early '70s. Living in a country that still brought chills to any American with the memories of Nazi Germany, Pat and her husband confronted the juxtapositions of post-war Germany and the fears of *if* and *when* he might be sent to Vietnam. While it was easy to relate to their newly-married struggles, I felt the silent wounds of the Vietnam Era rising to the surface once again. This time, though, healing came in her beauty to connect with any reader.

—Suzanne Robinson

Curse of Interesting Times expertly weaves together a newly-wed couples' love, the culture-shock of military life in Germany, and the events and pop culture of the Vietnam Conflict. The intimate details of the book gave me insight into the impact that this war had on university students, military husbands and their wives, and the citizens in countries that hosted military bases. It's a studied look at an important era in American history.

—Connie Shoemaker, author of *The Good Daughter:*
Secrets, Life Stories, and Healing
and *Taste the Sweetness Later*

What a journey Patricia Ann Paul has taken us on in this cleverly-written narrative of her experiences with her American soldier husband in Germany during the Viet Nam War—a refreshingly different perspective of that newly-revisited conflict.

—Bill Ward, author of *Beyond the River*
—*Stories of Life Near the Arkansas*

I love the way *Curse of Interesting Times, a* story of war and family, comes full circle in Germany. I felt like I was there with Pat and John in their tiny apartment in Germany and on their travels in post-World War II Germany during the Cold War. Such a frank and touching love story, and what an affirming way to end the book!
—Sally Walling

The Age *was* Aquarius, and no matter what else was going on in their life at that time, in the background loomed the war, the unwinnable Vietnam War. The author, Patricia Ann Paul, with her student husband, John, squarely faced their options with surprising results.
—Joyce Rovetta

CURSE of INTERESTING TIMES

A Vietnam-Era Memoir

Patricia Ann Paul

**Amity
Bridge
Books**

All rights reserved. Published in the United States by
Amity Bridge Books
Littleton, Colorado

CURSE OF INTERESTING TIMES:
A Vietnam-Era Memoir

Print ISBN: 978-0-9864253-2-5

EISBN: 978-0-9864253-3-2

Library of Congress Control Number: 2018900731

Dedication

To my best friend, husband, father of my sons:
Thanks for all our years together,
Cursed and uncursed,
Interesting and uninteresting.

Epigraph

There is an old Chinese curse which says
"May he live in interesting times."
Like it or not, we live in interesting times.
They are times of danger and uncertainty.
—Senator Robert F Kennedy 1966

Table of Contents

UNIVERSITY OF IOWA AND BEYOND

Prologue

◆

What If . . . ?

In October of 2006, on a day stolen from the inevitable approach of winter, I walk the National Mall in Washington, DC, with my friend Emily. A gentle breeze riffles my hair and skitters the brightly colored leaves across the still-green grass. While the air feels cool and invigorating against my face, the sun warms my back. It's a glorious fall day, one of those great-day-to-be-alive kind of days.

Emily and I make our way across 17th Street to the imposing World War II Memorial whose grandeur aptly venerates the courage of "The Greatest Generation." On the Freedom Wall, four thousand stars represent the 400,000 Americans who lost their lives in service to their country, and an inscription declares to us: HERE WE MARK THE PRICE OF FREEDOM. The brilliant sunshine plays in the fountains of the Rainbow Pool which separates the two pavilions representing the Atlantic and Pacific theaters of war. Fifty-six majestic granite pillars, one for each of the country's states and territories during that time, glorify what author Studs Terkel called The Good War.

Leaving the World War II Memorial, Emily and I continue our trek following a small sign indicating the way to the Vietnam Memorial down a winding path through shrubs and trees. Soon we find ourselves almost at

Constitution Avenue, the northern perimeter of the Mall, and think we have somehow missed the Memorial. As we discuss turning back, I catch a glimpse behind some foliage of what appears to be the low end of a retaining wall, less than a foot high. "What can it be?" I wonder and forge ahead not realizing what I am seeing. The shrubbery opens to reveal a black granite wall rising from the grass, inscribed with lists and lists of names, stretching into the distance. Then I spot the flowers and framed photos leaning against the base. The closest of the many pictures, a sepia portrait of a boy hardly beginning to shave with wavy hair brushed to the side, triggers the image of John's high school graduation picture, also an innocent young face in sepia, with no wrinkles, no jowls, unlike the 60-something John I know today. But for destiny, that boy in the photo, propped against the wall, could have been John.

Emotion slams me. Tears develop into sobs. I slump onto the grass and weep overwhelmed with thankfulness for my precious family, my sons, their wives, and those adorable grandchildren who run to greet me arms outstretched for a hug, my spark of immortality. At the same time, I feel embarrassed by the memory of my friend and classmate Fred Trumbull, a draftee like John. He went down in a helicopter crash leaving his parents not only without their only child, but also without grandchildren. Over 58,000 boys died in that conflict. Guilt overwhelms me. What a sniveler! Why do I deserve to grieve? But in spite of myself, I do.

Each sob releases some of the emotional undertow of those years. In time of war loving is risky business. The fear of the draft and then of Vietnam, of being a young widow, never abated from the time of our engagement in 1967 until John's army discharge December 29, 1970. Will he be drafted? Will he be sent to Nam? Will he face combat? A love can be mangled, blown to bits, missing in action, dead or disabled. Even when the Fickle Finger of Fate sent John to Germany, we discovered that transfer orders to Nam came for individuals and for entire companies. The Elephant in the room was Fear. He breathed down the back of my neck and tapped me on the shoulder saying, "Hey, remember! You and that guy! You're mortal." No assurances. No safety, no respite, until discharge. We never knew what tomorrow might bring.

Carried away by my memories, I forgot my friend Emily, now an Australian, but originally Irish with Old World stoicism and scant familiarity with the Vietnam Conflict. At first she gives me space to pull myself together. Then she comforts me, offers a tissue.

Flummoxed when neither strategy succeeds, she simply asks, "Pat, what's happening?"

I blubber the words: "What if . . . ?" I couldn't say the rest out loud.

When you came, you were like
red wine and honey,
And the taste of you burnt my mouth
with its sweetness.
Now you are like morning bread,
Smooth and pleasant.
I hardly taste you at all for I know your savor,
But I am completely nourished.
—Amy Lowell, "The Decade" 1919

It seems to me most strange
that men should fear;
Seeing that death, a necessary end,
Will come when it will come.
—William Shakespeare,
Julius Caesar 1599

To become spring, means accepting the
risk of winter. To become presence, means
accepting the risk of absence.
—Antoine de Saint-Exupéry,
Manon Ballerina 2007

DCAS Vietnam Conflict Extract File record counts by CASUALTY CATEGORY (as of April 29, 2008)

Casualty Category	Number of Records
ACCIDENT	9,107
DECLARED DEAD	1,201
DIED OF WOUNDS	5,299
HOMICIDE	236
ILLNESS	938
KILLED IN ACTION	40,934
PRESUMED DEAD (BODY REMAINS RECOVERED)	32
PRESUMED DEAD (BODY REMAINS NOT RECOVERED)	91
SELF-INFLICTED	382
Total Records	58,220

—US National Archives April 29, 2008

BOOK ONE

◆━━━━◆

UNIVERSITY OF IOWA

Vietnam Conflict Escalates: 1964-1967

August 2–7, 1964: After complaining about attacks from South Vietnamese and American gunboats patrolling off their coast in the Gulf of Tonkin, the North Vietnamese attack the USS Maddox in international waters causing no damage and no casualties. The Maddox reports a second attack two days later although evidence is inconclusive. The US Congress passes the Gulf of Tonkin Resolution empowering President Johnson to defend South Vietnam but stops short of a declaration of war.

December 31, 1964: During 1964 US troop levels in Vietnam reach 23,300 Americans. Since 1954 when President Eisenhower sent the first military advisors to Vietnam, 416 of them have died.

March 8, 1965: US Marines, 3500 strong, arrive in Vietnam. Not military advisors, they are the first combat troops.

July 28, 1965: President Lyndon Johnson announces in a press conference that he is more than doubling the draft to provide troops for Vietnam. He also indicates he is not calling up Army Reserve units. Until he leaves office, he continues to follow this policy of mobilization through the draft instead of through Reserve units.

August, 1965: Pete Seeger releases a single 45 rpm recording of his anti-war song "Where Have All the Flowers Gone?"

August 31, 1965: Targeting the Vietnam Conflict protesters who are publicly burning their draft cards, the US Congress criminalizes the destruction of draft cards with possible penalties of up to five years in prison and up to $10,000 in fines.

October 20, 1965: Stephen Lynn Smith, a student at the University of Iowa, burns his draft card at a rally at the Memorial Union. He is arrested, found guilty, and sentenced to three years probation.

December 15–16, 1965–1968: In Des Moines, Iowa, three students are suspended for wearing black armbands to protest the war. Based on the students' freedom of speech, the US Supreme Court agrees to hear the case, Tinker v Des Moines Independent Community School District.

December 31, 1965: US troop levels in Vietnam reach 184,300 Americans; 1,928 die.

March 25–26, 1966: The National Coordinating Committee to End the War in Vietnam organizes the Days of International Protest with demonstrations in New York City, Boston, Philadelphia, Washington, Chicago, Detroit, San Francisco, Oklahoma City, Ottawa, London, Oslo, Stockholm, Lyon, and Tokyo. In New York alone 20,000 participate.

March 31, 1966–January 24, 1968: In defiance of the law against destroying draft cards, draft card burnings multiply around the country. When student David O'Brien burns his draft card on the steps of the South Boston Courthouse, the US Supreme Court hears his case addressing the question of whether the law infringes on his right of freedom of speech. A decision is expected soon.

December 31, 1966: US troop levels in Vietnam reach 385,300 Americans; 6,350 die.

October 16, 1967: The National Mobilization Committee to End the War in Vietnam (The Mobe) organizes a day of war protest in 30 cities across the country; some 1,400 protesters burn their draft cards.

October 1967: Arlo Guthrie releases his album Alice's Restaurant, including a narrative song satirizing his rejection from the draft, unfit due to a conviction for littering.

October 21, 1967: One hundred thousand demonstrators march to the Lincoln Memorial and roughly half continue to the Pentagon to protest against the war.

November 30, 1967: President Johnson "releases" Secretary of Defense Robert S McNamara from his position after he publicly expresses his concerns about the war.

December 31, 1967: US troop levels in Vietnam reach 485,600 Americans; 11,363 die.

January 30, 1968: After repeated reports from American leaders that victory is in sight, North Vietnam during their Tet holiday launches simultaneous attacks in major cities, towns, and military bases throughout South Vietnam. Although a military victory for the US, it becomes a psychological turning point.

February 27, 1968: After returning from covering the Tet Offensive in Vietnam, CBS news anchor Walter Cronkite, referred to as the most trusted man in America, ends his evening broadcast stating, "It seems now more certain than ever that the bloody experience of Vietnam is to end in a stalemate."

1

President Johnson's Speech

March 31, 1968: A Gallup Poll reports that President Johnson has a 36 percent approval rating on the conduct of his office and 26 percent approval of his handling of the war.

March 31, 1968: President Johnson states in a nationwide television broadcast that the US is willing to enter peace negotiations. He stuns the nation announcing he will not seek reelection in 1968.

"June 15, your wedding is June 15th? You won't be there." That's what the old bat at the Jasper County draft board told John when he called first thing the morning of April 1, 1968.

"I won't be there?"

"You say you're graduating the week before?"

"Yes. Graduation is on the 7th."

"You'll lose your student deferment on graduation day."

"And I could be drafted that fast . . . in just eight days?"

"Son, I wouldn't recommend a lot of fancy wedding plans for June 15th." John just hung up. He gulped for air.

That call confirming that he would be drafted, could become cannon fodder in Vietnam, ended our childhood and began our loss of innocence. Our parents' sheltered nurturing could not reach far enough to protect us now.

Actually, it began the evening before this fateful phone call, after dinner on March 31st, at Alpha Gamma Chi, my sorority house at the University of Iowa. I came downstairs in search of John who would be finishing his houseboy duties in the kitchen. I caught sight of him striding out of the swinging kitchen door like Matt Dillon swaggering out of the Long Branch Saloon. After a quick glance to each side confirmed we were alone, he pulled me close for a forbidden kiss. I tried to brush the dangling Elvis-like curl from his forehead before we joined the others in the chapter room.

Usually a quiet place during study hours, the room quickly filled with girls and some drenched boyfriends, who came out in spite of the rain and hail to hear what President Johnson might say about the war in his televised address to the nation. A few in the group attempted light-hearted banter which met with anxious titters, but a somber mood prevailed because the stakes were high for these young men. John and I remained quiet, focused on finding an empty place for two. We had to settle for the hard linoleum-tiled floor with our backs against the slick vinyl turquoise couch. With my right hand I gripped John's hand tightly. With my left, I pressed my thumb against the back of my engagement ring, as if keeping it firmly in place could keep my fiancé firmly in place beside me.

We focused on the blond cabinet-style TV, doors spread wide, waiting to see if the President's speech might affect us. Even though we were graduating this spring, John had been accepted into grad school in the fall, so we hoped he would continue to be deferred from the Vietnam draft. United States involvement in Vietnam had begun in the 1950s under President Eisenhower, who provided military training and equipment to the South Vietnamese involving less than 800 US military personnel. Those numbers had grown somewhat during the Kennedy Administration but had escalated to nearly 500,000 during the Presidency of Lyndon Johnson, both Presidents influenced by their Secretary of Defense, Robert S McNamara. Many Americans believed the war to be a necessary defense during the Cold War to restrain the communist governments of the Soviet Union and China, backers of our North Vietnamese enemy. They believed in the *Domino Theory*, that if one country fell to communism, the others around it, in this case, all of Southeast Asia, would follow.

The fear of communism which included the nuclear threat of the Soviets had been part of our childhood. At school we did "duck and cover" drills hiding under our desks although no one believed that could provide real protection from a nuclear weapon. My best friend Fran's father, who headed the local civil defense effort, built a bomb shelter under his backyard and stocked it with bottled water and canned goods. In this climate of fear, I well remember not being able to sleep during the Cuban Missile Crisis of 1962, my junior year in high school, thinking I would not live to graduate. Reading novels about nuclear annihilation, such as Nevil Shute's *On the Beach,* even more chilling in the film version, convinced me that mankind was doomed. The fear of communism was palpable in American society.

Even so, many Americans believed that the United States was interfering in a civil war between North and South Vietnam. Americans felt no threat from a former

French colony, now a small, undeveloped country in far away Southeast Asia, a country which many Americans had never heard of before the conflict. Vietnam had no nukes. Instead, folks opposed to the war, referred to as *doves*, feared that the Gulf of Tonkin Resolution passed by Congress empowering President Johnson to defend South Vietnam, in fact, had been provoked by the US. The failure of the Congress to actually declare war supported those suspicions. And, it eventually became apparent to Americans that corruption permeated the government of the South.

As the numbers of military personnel escalated, the number of draftees and casualties increased, and so did opposition to the war. By October of 1967, around 100,000 anti-war demonstrators made the trip to Washington, DC, to protest at the Lincoln Memorial and outside the windows of Secretary McNamara at the Pentagon. In November President Johnson "released" McNamara, who had grown publicly discouraged with the progress and possible success of the war. Americans for the first time ever were viewing the horrific images of war in their own homes via television. Soldiers, mistrusting their government's reasons for sending them to Vietnam, began using drugs and mutinied against officers.

For our leaders the Vietnam Conflict had become a point of pride: the US had never lost a war. They didn't regard the stalemate that resulted in North and South Korea as a loss. Was it right to continue a war, to continue the loss of life, just because the country's leaders didn't want to admit they had made a mistake? The pro-war bumper stickers of their supporters, the hawks, proliferated on the streets of America declaring My Country, Right or Wrong and America, Love It or Leave It.

Yet the popular folk music of the time amplified the protest movement. Iconic singer and song-writer Pete Seeger, blacklisted during the McCarthy era for refusing to name communist sympathizers, liked to quote Plato: "It's very dangerous to allow the wrong kind of music in the Republic." Indeed, his song "Where Have All the Flowers Gone?" in protest of the Vietnam Conflict was translated into many languages around the world and recorded by numerous celebrities and groups worldwide including Marlene Dietrich.

In the mid-fifties, before Vietnam, Seeger wrote an original version of the song, only three verses, as a question and answer. He began, "Where have all the flowers gone . . . picked by young girls." The second verse asked, "Where have all the young girls gone . . . gone to husbands." And he ended, "Where have all the husbands gone . . . gone to soldiers." The song was published and recorded that way until around 1960 when camp counsellor Joe Hickerson with his campers added two more verses to complete the circle. In their verses the soldiers had "Gone to graveyards" and the graveyards had "Gone to flowers," thus completing the circle. With Vietnam heating up in 1964, Seeger released his 45 rpm of the song with Hickerson's additional verses, and he included it on an album of his greatest hits in 1967. Wikipedia lists around 50 recorded versions in English, German, French, Russian, and numerous other languages as diverse as Bengali, as the song caught on with the war protest movement.

This anti-war sentiment hung over the Presidency of Lyndon Baines Johnson as he faced opposition in the Presidential primaries from Senators Robert Kennedy and Eugene McCarthy. On the very day of Johnson's televised address, March 31, 1968, a Gallup Poll showed three of every four Americans disagreed with Johnson on the war.

Then, on the TV, the traditional voice-over grabbed our attention: "Ladies and Gentlemen, the President of the United States."

Johnson began in a serious, almost funereal tone, in his soft Texas drawl, "Good evening, my fellow Americans." He outlined plans for a more conciliatory strategy which he hoped would bring North Vietnam to the negotiating table.

Then he switched to a plea for unity explaining, "The ultimate strength of our country . . . will lie in the unity of our people. And in these times as in times before, it is true that a house divided against itself by the spirit of faction, of party, of region, of religion, of race, is a house that cannot stand."

Johnson continued acknowledging, "There is division in the American house now . . ." and concluded by dropping his own bomb. "With America's sons in the fields far away, . . . I do not believe that I should devote an hour or a day of my time to any personal partisan causes. . . . Accordingly, I shall not seek, and I will not accept, the nomination of my party for another term as your President."

While Johnson's renunciation of his own political future stunned the world, John and I remember being most stunned about our own marital future. As we remember it, that was the night we grasped the reality that on graduation day, John would lose his student draft deferment, his protection from the horrific scenes of Vietnam we saw on TV, in spite of his admission to grad school for next fall. Graduate students would no longer be deferred from the military draft. His phone call to the local draft board the next morning would confirm it.

We of the Kennedy and Johnson administrations who participated in the decisions on Vietnam acted according to what we thought were the principles and traditions of this nation. We made our decisions in light of those values. Yet we were wrong, terribly wrong. We owe it to future generations to explain.
—Robert S McNamara,
In Retrospect: The Tragedy and Lessons of Vietnam 1995

This is the story we have told innumerable times through the years. It is the way we both remember it. But when I searched the internet for the text of Johnson's speech before writing this chapter, I could find nothing about eliminating the graduate school deferment. I was stunned. It was like discovering that some giant had picked up my childhood home and set it down on the other side of town. I read the text over and over again. It did stress the need for Americans to share equally in the sacrifices, but never specifically mentioned the graduate school deferment. Some did regard that exemption as the rich buying their way out of serving; however, we never felt like *the rich*. John's mother provided his college education by leaving retirement to teach kindergarten half days. She endorsed her paycheck each month and mailed it to him. He stretched it with a variety of part-time jobs, such as sorority houseboy, high school janitor, or clerking at Montgomery Ward. Toward the end of each month when I knew he was broke, I bought groceries, bread, peanut butter and jelly, cherry Jello, and bananas to surprise him at his apartment with the fixings for lunch. He thought I was nesting.

Rich or poor, how did the graduate school deferment disappear? Further research revealed that Johnson recommended that change over a year earlier on March 6, 1967. Then, when Congress passed an extension to the Selective Service Act on June 30, 1967, Johnson issued Executive Order 11360 eliminating deferments for postgraduate study, except for those in medical and dental programs. It was to take effect a year later, the summer of 1968, the summer we were to graduate and marry. We must have known that!

What were we thinking? Probably that night we had hoped Johnson would announce an end to US involvement in the war or an end to the draft or at least the beginning of real peace negotiations—any progress toward ending the war. Or, most likely, perhaps we couldn't believe he would implement his executive order and actually do away with the graduate school deferment. We must have hoped for a continuing deferment. As John Lennon sang in "Beautiful Boy," a song to his son Sean,

"Life is what happens to you when you're busy making other plans." Somehow, we had been in denial. We had not accepted it irrevocably as fact until Johnson's speech, March 31, 1968. John's draft status 2-S (student deferment) would end in two months on June 7, graduation day. It would not continue for graduate school. His new status would become 1-A (available immediately), and he would be drafted into the army before our wedding set for June 15.

2

JP

So, who is this John? What about John set my head and heart spinning with euphoria? Just a few months ago my best friend saw a picture of him from our newlywed days.

Her response, "Why, Pat, he was hot!"

That should have been a compliment, but with the shock in her tone, I felt a little insulted. Why didn't she think I would have had a *hot* young husband?

So, maybe I need to start with me? Who was I nearly fifty years ago? I was an egghead who mostly lived in the books I carried everywhere. I was more mature than the boys around me in high school which didn't help. Never mind that I had no idea how to talk to a boy. I remember reading the encyclopedia entry on automobile engines because I thought it might give me something to talk about with a boy I liked who had just gotten his driver's license. Thank God, the opportunity never arose for that conversation!

Fran, my best friend, the one whose father built a backyard bomb shelter, was a curly-haired redhead with crystalline blue eyes and a face without a single freckle, the color of Ivory soap. She was a cheerleader, on the Homecoming Court, and then Sweetheart Queen for the Valentine's dance. I was the one who did her hair before the big dance teasing her red curls into the popular bouffant style. Sometimes I had a date myself, and sometimes not. I was the nice girl who made good grades. She was the heart throb. I was the best friend.

I hoped it would get better in college, that the boys would grow up. Well, they did. At the University of Iowa, one of the nation's highest-ranked party schools, they grew from clumsy attempts to find something to drink and a girl to help them explore social boundaries to firmly securing a supply of alcohol and regular sexual activity. So, the early years of college were even worse for me.

In the fall of 1964, my freshman year in college, my best friend in the dorm was another blue-eyed, redhead, this one named Patti, same as me. Our dorm mates referred to her as Patti with an *i* and to me as Patty with a *y*. One Saturday night I was still up when she came home from a blind date with a freshman fraternity pledge to a "woodsy," supposedly a campfire with guitarists and folk songs, definitely in the woods after dark, although the fire wasn't the only way to keep warm.

"Oh, you've got something on your cheek," I said.

She stepped toward the mirror in my room, turning her face to examine her cheek. "Oooh, that's what I was afraid of. It's a burn. I need to wash it out," she replied heading out the door and down the hall toward the bathroom.

"A burn . . . a burn? How did you get a burn . . . on your cheek?" I inquired trailing along behind her, acting more like her mother than her friend.

Splashing water on her face, she said, "Well, he was smoking, and he tried to kiss me. I think he'd had too much beer to get the timing right. Everybody was lying on blankets, spread out, all over the place, mostly out of sight from each other, and making-out like crazy. Not good for a first date." She turned to face me, "Why did I go? I should have known."

I mentally filed it as a lesson about university life and resolved to avoid woodsies as if I would ever have the opportunity. But you'll never guess what. The next weekend she accepted another date with him.

"Are you crazy? Your cheek isn't even healed yet!" I exclaimed, my mind blown.

"Well, actually, I can't explain it, but he's kind of sweet."

So, she gave him another chance, just the two of them, no beer, no woodsy, and especially no expectations from older fraternity actives to "score." She decided she liked him.

They began dating. I met him later that fall in the lobby of our dorm, Burge Hall. I still remember the first time. He had this Caesar haircut which was all the rage, natural curls that dangled onto his forehead, a crooked smile, half cocky and half shy. You just knew he was every teacher's nightmare, the kid who cracked up the class and, in spite of herself, the teacher, too. He and Patti became a couple. Sometimes when I had a date, we doubled. But the summer of 1966 before their junior year, he was heartbroken when she decided to move on. Being used to the role of best friend, I spent a lot of time consoling him, becoming his new best friend.

This best-friend thing continued through fall semester and into the new year. We were studying together frequently. I think we both had to realize that we were intentionally choosing to study at the student union in order to "accidentally" bump into each other. On

21

Valentine's Day of 1967, our junior year, it was 65 degrees in Iowa City, a record high in the middle of February. We decided to ditch the books and take a walk in the park. The trees stood leafless surrounded by brown grass, but the sunshine and warmth tricked us into a case of spring fever. It played out like a movie scene, a stolen kiss, a boundary crossed. We entered a new world. The whole best-friend thing ended that afternoon, not without trepidation, as we knew, if it didn't work out, we were risking the loss of our best friend.

With him, she was at ease; her skin felt as though it was her right size. . . . It seemed so natural, to talk to him about odd things. She had never done that before. The trust, so sudden and yet so complete, and the intimacy, frightened her.
—Chimamanda Ngozi Adichie,
Americanah 2013

"What does really matter?" I asked.
She looked at me as though wondering if she could trust me with some immense secret. Finally she said, "Having someone to love. Being compassionate. Being fully alive everyday so that you really see and hear and smell and feel things."
—Jonathan Hull,
Losing Julia 2000

It was a wild time, falling in love. I know why they say *falling* in love. It's a similar sensation to being a loose leaf, free in the breeze, the exhilaration of floating downward, helplessly caught by the tug of gravity, yet never hitting the ground.

We reveled in the music of our times dancing at The Hawk on Friday nights, shouting along to The Stones: "I Can't Get No Satisfaction;" The Beatles: "Hard Day's Night"; The Doors: "G-l-o-r-i-a"! Yes, we were hot! On Saturday nights I flushed the abstinence of my Methodist upbringing buying beer for us at the neighborhood grocery, ironically named John's Place, around the corner from John's apartment. It was infamous for not carding under-age buyers, although I was 21. John still had a few more months before his 21st. So, legally speaking, I was contributing to the delinquency of a minor, but I think that minor was contributing to my delinquency.

Besides having fun it was a time of making delightful discoveries about one another. One weekend I took him home to meet my parents. While we took advantage of the quiet living room to study, sitting close together on Mom's new, silk, avocado-green sofa, he inadvertently dropped a blue marker which rolled under him leaving a permanent stain. Thinking he had blown our relationship, embarrassed and chagrined to his core, he went to his room and shut the door. Eventually Mom took him a coke and some cookies to entice him back out. She could tell he had been crying, and she couldn't control her sympathetic reaction. By the next day, she had flipped the sofa cushion.

When she saw John's puzzled gaze as he tried to find the offending blue mark, with her most angelic expression, she told him a bold-faced lie, "I got it out with stain remover." It was John's "red badge of courage." Although wounded, he survived meeting his future in laws. A year later on another visit, now virtually a member of the family, it dawned on him to lift the cushion and check the other side. There it was: the blue streak. He confronted Mom, who to my knowledge had never lied in her life. Hopelessly embarrassed, she avoided his eyes muttering, "It's only a cushion."

Another weekend he took me to the farm and to the home where he had lived since birth. Built in 1914 by his maternal grandparents, the Burtons, it was a two-story, arts-and-crafts house with walnut woodwork, walnut paneling, and walnut columns. Grandpa Burton, still living and 88 years old, occupied the main floor with his widowed-daughter, John's Aunt Sara, who took care of Grandpa. John's parents, Vesta and William, lived in the remodeled upstairs apartment created during the housing shortage of World War II. It was supposed to be temporary, but the arrangement suited everyone and became permanent.

I felt the warmth and support that he had experienced growing up in a three-generation household. Outside, I still remember the fragile green shoots of corn and beans in neat rows barely piercing the rich, black soil. The frisky, but awkward, toy-sized lambs, the symbol of spring's promise for new life and another year, frolicked irresistibly. I had been a city girl from the big town of Bettendorf, Iowa, but hand-feeding an orphaned lamb from a baby bottle, I couldn't resist the allure of rural life.

Being part of a close family was essential for both of us. As winter dissolved and the real spring emerged, I could tell he was the real thing: what he saw as best for me was what he made best for himself. As the relationship developed in seriousness, so did it develop physically. The lyrics of one of our favorite Beatles' songs, "I Want to Hold Your Hand," captured it for us: "And when I touch you I feel happy inside." As I was still a virgin, John insisted that not change until I was ready. The continuing relationship was most important to him. This was a huge decision before The Pill and legal abortion. Other contraceptives, while available, were not fool-proof, and who is more foolish than a couple in love? The consequences were enormous. For a white, middle-class, Protestant girl from a small town in Iowa, a pregnancy before marriage meant at best forced marriage or shame and ostracism, even by one's own family. Never mind the responsibility of a precious new life! Single mothers were virtually unheard of and certainly not from upright, church-going families. So making this decision meant trust with a capital *T*. It meant knowing that John was with me for good, would not walk away. That a forced marriage, if necessary, would be a blessing, not a disaster, however inconvenient before we graduated.

When I finally decided I was ready, we were ready, I had to tell him in the light of day, not in the heat of the moment. Even then he was so concerned that he might lose his best friend, he made me think about it while we were apart over spring break, 10 whole days. He didn't want me to have any regrets. Nice guys do not finish last. I identified with those new lambs on the farm, kicking up my heels in the springtime. That was April. When he found out I loved daffodils, he took off for Mercy Hospital, just down the street from my sorority, where they bought donated blood. He used the payment to surprise me with a bouquet the color of spring sunshine. By May we were planning a wedding, not until after graduation a year away, but it was definitely on for June of 1968.

We both got lucky. I was left-brained, analytical, organized, a list-maker and calendar-bound super planner. He was creative, right-brained, intuitive, artistic, witty and spontaneous. In me he got a serious student and, henceforth, adjusted his study habits, resulting in a meteoric rise in his GPA, enough to plan on grad school. I got a sweet, but rakish, fun-loving guy who helped me lighten up and enjoy life. Someone who has always cared for me, emotionally as well as physically. And besides being in love, we were still best friends . . . are still best friends. The union has been stronger than either individual.

A big part of a healthy relationship is . . . can you sacrifice for your partner for the good of the relationship as a whole?
—Joshua Hook,
psychologist and professor,
University of North Texas 2016

3

A Rifle in the Rice Paddies

April 3, 1968: One thousand young men around the country illegally turn in their draft cards to protest the Vietnam Conflict.

April 4, 1968: In Memphis, Tennessee, James Earl Ray assassinates Rev Martin Luther King, Jr, leader of the American civil rights movement and winner of the 1964 Nobel Peace Prize. Deadly riots spread in cities throughout the US.

April 29, 1968: Hair: The American Tribal Love-Rock Musical *opens on Broadway and runs for 1,750 performances. The main character Claude must decide whether to resist the draft like his friends or serve in Vietnam as his parents wish.* Hair *is the first Broadway production to include nude actors, both male and female, on stage together.*

April–May 1968: Protesters occupy five buildings at Columbia University.

May 17, 1968: Protesters led by Philip Berrigan and his brother, Daniel, enter a draft board office in Catonsville, Maryland, remove records, and set them afire outside with homemade napalm in front of reporters and onlookers.

May 27, 1968: In the United States v O'Brien, the US Supreme Court finds that the federal law prohibiting draft card destruction, in this case burning, is not an unconstitutional infringement of David O'Brien's freedom of speech.

June 6, 1968: Sirhan Sirhan, a Jordanian, assassinates Senator Robert F Kennedy, brother of former President John F Kennedy, immediately after RFK's California Democratic Presidential primary victory speech.

I need to explain. Why didn't we want John to serve? Were we pacifists, conscientious objectors? No, I can't say that we were. After World War II, when our parents' generation defeated Hitler and stopped the Holocaust, it was hard to say that war was never justified. Then, was John a draft-dodger?

On university campuses the draft hung over the heads of the male students. It was the task of The Selective Service System, an independent agency of the United States government, to obtain the men necessary to fight in Vietnam. Although we have an entirely professional armed forces now with no draft, in the time of past wars, our country drafted troops to meet the demand for military personnel: soldiers. Still today all males must register with the Selective Service within 30 days of their 18th birthday in case a military emergency would require resuming the draft.

The draft had become an ever-tightening noose for young, healthy males in the US. In 1963 before the Gulf of Tonkin Resolution, married men and all full-time students were exempt from the draft which had summoned 119,265 men that year to serve in the armed forces. By 1965 as the demand for troops increased following the Gulf of Tonkin Resolution, President

Johnson by Executive Order rescinded the exemption for married men without children. The number of draftees more than doubled. By 1966 that number jumped again to 382,010, and it remained between 200-300,000 for the next four years.

But a male student who was enrolled full-time and maintained good-standing academically in any institution of higher learning did not have to serve until he had completed his program. That included vocational schools, community colleges, undergraduate and graduate colleges, and universities. Yet all students knew they must serve once they completed their education. Their status was temporary, more accurate when stated as a *deferment*. Their service was deferred until they graduated.

Regardless, the raw rift caused by the draft intensified as it affected more and more male students and their loved ones. For sons of the wealthy, continuing in school full time and concentrating on making grades was fairly straight forward. However, not everyone had a lawyer daddy who could provide a free ride. Many students received some financial help from home but had to augment that with part-time and summer jobs. Others received no financial help. They depended on financial aid or loans from the university or on working or most often all of the above.

So, what happened if a student didn't have enough money for tuition and living expenses? He had to work more hours, but he couldn't take fewer classes or let his grades fall. He could end up with a rifle in the rice paddies.

Or what about the kid who didn't know what he wanted to be when he grew up, most freshmen didn't, and flunked first semester engineering classes? He had to make up those hours in summer school. But then what happened to his ability to pay tuition from the proceeds of his summer job? He could end up with a rifle in the rice paddies.

Of course, any student who dropped out for any reason or who couldn't keep his grades up for any reason, also, lost his deferment. Never mind a student who fell behind due to transferring schools or changing majors. He could end up with a rifle in the rice paddies.

Many young men struggled to stay in school. They couldn't work for a semester and go to school for a semester working in a restaurant for their board and driving a hearse at night for their room in the mortuary, like my father did. He would have ended up with a rifle in the rice paddies.

Every young American male, age 18 or over, was required to carry his draft card, physically similar to a driver's license, at all times. It bore the registrant's identifying information, the date and place of registration, and his Selective Service number, which indicated his state of registration, local board, birth year, and his classification. As student frustration with the uncertainties and fear of the draft grew, young men destroyed their draft cards in protest. The card itself being mostly symbolic, it changed nothing since those records also existed in each selective service board at the county courthouse. The only real consequence: it did make a point in public. In reaction Congress criminalized the destruction of draft cards on August 31, 1965, with penalties including a five-year prison term and up to $10,000 in fines.

The following March student David O'Brien and three friends burned their draft cards on the steps of the South Boston Courthouse. Immediately arrested, O'Brien, who defended himself in court, stated his reasons to the jury: ". . . so that other people would reevaluate their positions with Selective Service, with the armed forces, and reevaluate their place in the culture of today, to hopefully consider my position." Subsequently convicted, his case was accepted by the Supreme Court and tried in January of 1968. The question: Was the law an unconstitutional infringement of O'Brien's First Amendment right to the freedom of speech? A decision was expected by summer.

Meanwhile, in October of 1967, Arlo Guthrie, the son of Woody Guthrie, the beloved Depression-era folk music artist and writer of "This Land Is My Land, This Land Is Your Land," inspired the protestors with his own anti-draft song entitled "The Alice's Restaurant Massacree." It provided a satirical monologue of a true story from the younger Guthrie's life. On Thanksgiving 1965 he received a citation for littering which led to the Selective Service rejecting him for the draft because of his conviction for that crime. The irony in the story is, as Guthrie sings it: "I'm sittin' here on the Group W bench 'cause you want to know if I'm moral enough to join the Army—burn women, kids, houses and villages—after bein' a litterbug?" The song ends with Guthrie inviting his audience to sing along, resist the draft, and bring an end to the war. A movie based on the song was in production by 1968.

Were we hippies, pot-smoking protesters, scruffy draft-card burners? To this day, I have never smoked a joint, not even now it's legal in Colorado. Knowing what I know now, I wish I could say we had protested. Secretary of Defense McNamara's apology for his involvement in the war published in 1995, *In Retrospect,* provided vindication for the protesters, draft-card burners, and Canadian draft dodgers. I regret that we, like McNamara, were not able to make better sense of the complexities of our own time.

Were we informed about Ho Chi Minh and the history of Vietnam that led to the Civil War? I wish I could say we knew more. Like most Americans we had never heard of Vietnam until the US began fighting there. Gradually we developed a vague knowledge that Vietnam had been a French colonial country, that the Vietnamese had managed to gain independence from the French, and that, subsequently, a civil war had developed between the communist Vietnamese, mainly in the north, and rival powers, mainly in the south. We didn't know, for example, that the Vietnamese Declaration of Independence, written by Ho Chi Minh before they split into the North and the South, was modeled on ours. We didn't know at that time that the government in the South was corrupt or that civilians were dying due to *democide*, the execution of political opponents by their own government. The professor of political science who coined that term, RJ Rummel, was renowned for the Democratic Peace Theory that democracies don't go to war with each other. Regarding democide in Vietnam, his research estimated that US troops executed 6,000 South Vietnamese civilians in addition to the 89,000 killed by their own government.

We did know the Domino Theory, that if one Southeast Asian country fell to communism, the rest would follow. The United States was fighting a conventional war against communism in Vietnam because it could not fight the real communist powers of the Cold War: the USSR and China. That would have involved nuclear weapons and the nuclear annihilation that we had grown up fearing. We had survived the Cuban Missile Crisis. The Cubans moved the missiles, and life went on even though the Cold War continued to cause fear in America.

Or were we just plain selfish and unpatriotic? That's what many of our parents' generation thought. We were the Baby Boomers, the children of the Greatest Generation, those who made the sacrifices required to win World War II. They had saved the world from fascism and stopped the Holocaust. Were our own fathers veterans? My father, Ken, as a married, but childless man of 31, enlisted during World War II, knowing he would be drafted soon. He hoped he might have more say in his assignment than if he waited to be drafted. After basic training, he received a medical discharge and never served after that. But he had enlisted.

John's father, William, being a married farmer with a child, John's older sister, was draft exempt during World War II and did not enlist. I begged him to let John help with the farm which would have given John an agricultural exemption, too. He wouldn't do it, he said, because of what the neighbors would think since he had stayed home during World War II. *What the neighbors would think?* We were talking about my husband's life, his only son's life!

I never really forgave him in his lifetime. I do realize now that he knew John would make a terrible farmer and the financial situation wouldn't have supported another family. I also came to understand the farm ethos around neighbors. Neighbors depended on each other to make hay, harvest the crop, take care of each other, whatever was needed. The farm community served as the social safety net. Cooperation and good standing meant survival. I was naive, and he had never overcome the shame he felt for his exemption during World War II.

So, was John in school just to avoid the draft? Definitely, not. Did we hope the war might end before John completed his education? Well, admittedly, yes. Did we think that likely? Well, not really. But that thought did provide hope. In most ways we more closely resembled the silent majority referred to by Nixon, just corn-fed, midwestern, square kids. John, although unable to control his wavy hair, wore a conservative haircut, trim around the ears and neck with no facial hair, and I still wore skirts to class and a Mary-Tyler-Moore flip hairdo.

What it came down to, nothing heroic, we were two scared kids! Did we believe in the Domino Theory? Well, it was only a theory. Who knew what would really happen? Would the war make a difference? Did we trust more in the politicians or in our own generation, the student protesters and especially the returning Vietnam veterans against the war? They had been there and didn't believe the war was valid or winnable? Interesting times: difficult to unravel what was really happening. What was right? What was wrong?

All men are created equal. They are endowed by their Creator with certain inalienable rights, among these are Life, Liberty, and the pursuit of Happiness.

This immortal statement was made in the Declaration of Independence of the United States of America in 1776. In a broader sense, this means: All the peoples on the earth are equal from birth, all the peoples have a right to live, to be happy and free.

The Declaration of the French Revolution made in 1791 on the Rights of Man and the Citizen also states: "All men are born free and with equal rights, and must always remain free and have equal rights." Those are undeniable truths.

Nevertheless, for more than eighty years, the French imperialists, abusing the standard of Liberty, Equality, and Fraternity, have violated our Fatherland and oppressed our fellow-citizens. They have acted contrary to the ideals of humanity and justice. In the field of politics, they have deprived our people of every democratic liberty.

[Following a list of grievances against the French similar to those listed in the Declaration of Independence of the United States of America against King George III of England, Ho ends with the following:]

For these reasons, we, members of the Provisional Government of the Democratic Republic of Vietnam, solemnly declare to the world that Vietnam has the right to be a free and independent country and in fact it is so already. The entire Vietnamese people are determined to mobilise [sic] all their physical and mental strength, to sacrifice their lives and property in order to safeguard their independence and liberty.

—Ho Chi Minh,
Declaration of Independence,
Republic of Vietnam 1945

So, here it was two months from graduation. What to do? You could go to Canada. You would be illegal, so holding a job beyond flipping burgers or laying sod, would not be in your future in spite of a college degree. If you ever crossed the border back into the US, you would be arrested for draft evasion which meant serious prison time. You could not go home—ever. For two kids just beginning to separate from close-knit families and just finishing college degrees, Canada was unimaginable.

You could enlist and supposedly have some choice in your assignment; however, everybody knew somebody who had signed up for radio school and ended up in the infantry in Nam. You could apply for Officer Candidate School which delayed your being drafted during the application process but required another year or more of service. Or, if you were really lucky, you could get into the National Guard and serve at home since President Johnson had made a decision not to call up National Guard units to fight in Vietnam. He didn't feel secure enough in his pursuit of the conflict to take guardsmen who tended to be older and established with families and careers. That might cause protest. Because they meant safety, guard openings were rare. Before the general population even knew they existed, politicians' sons snapped them up which explains some Vietnam veterans' anger at George W Bush during his campaign. Without connections snagging a National Guard opening required a lot of tilting at windmills. You heard about openings on the grapevine, never knowing whether they were real. To get one, you had to be there in person, pretty much first come, first served.

The most attractive choice to us, although in hindsight probably not a choice at all, seemed to be the National Guard. Sure enough, that weekend the rumor mill said there were openings in Fort Dodge, three hours from Iowa City. So, Monday morning John got up in the middle of the night to be in Fort Dodge before the recruiter's office opened because there was sure to be a line. I went to my classes, but no way could I concentrate. Afterward, I waited for John's return at the sorority house. I saw his turquoise and white Fairlane 500 pull into the driveway. He emerged, head bent, hunkered down inside his jacket against the sharp spring wind, both hands pushed deep inside his pockets. As he came around the corner of the car, he took a vicious kick at an offending stray piece of gravel sending it scuttling across the asphalt. He didn't have to say a word. He had cut three classes and used a tank of gas he couldn't afford only to find a dark office with a crude, handwritten note taped to the door: "Quota Filled."

So, the next week we tried a different tactic. John called the recruiter in Cedar Rapids to talk about applying for Officer Candidate School.

"Oh, yes. I can help you with that, but you need to understand that since the graduate school deferment is ending, the army OCS has way more applicants than we need. Even if you're accepted, you do your basic training and then there is a wait currently for eight, maybe nine months, before you start officer training school."

"Uh, and what do you do while you wait?" John asked.

"Whatever they need you to do, son."

Not a happy thought, but John made an appointment at 10:00, this time on Tuesday so he wouldn't miss the same classes. We assumed it would be pretty straight forward, drive to Cedar Rapids, only thirty minutes away, perhaps an interview, get the application packet. That's it!

Again, I waited. By noon John wasn't back. Maybe the guy really wanted to talk or maybe the appointment started late? The afternoon passed. Once again John walked in just in time for his houseboy duties at dinner.

Where had he been? Why? I tagged along behind him as he stomped toward the kitchen.

He slammed through the swinging door, turned and spat out his reply: "The recruiter never showed. I waited on the floor outside his office all day. I tried to review for my mid-term tomorrow, but I couldn't really keep my mind on it."

This pattern repeated and repeated. Active duty recruiters didn't return calls or didn't show up for appointments, and National Guard openings were always filled by the better-connected before regular folk could get there. April had passed, and May was the month before our June wedding. Despair set in.

At this point I thought I had best let my parents know that all the wedding plans might be for nothing. Dad, although not against the war, had his reservations about its conduct. The treatment of the draftees angered him never mind his fear that we would elope, and probably he was even more afraid of living with my mother if we did. So, he called his Congressman, probably the only time in his life. Indeed, Fred Schwengel, Congressman from Iowa's First District, arranged an appointment for John with a naval officer-candidate recruiter in Rock Island, Illinois, just across the Mississippi River from Bettendorf. The recruiter kept that appointment. John succeeded in applying for Navy OCS, a process that meanwhile required the draft board to hold him from induction. It would give us enough time to marry on June 15.

Parameters, Journal of the US Army War College

MOBILIZATION FOR THE VIETNAM WAR: A POLITICAL AND MILITARY CATASTROPHE

by JOHN D. STUCKEY and JOSEPH H. PISTORIUS 1985

The United States has never maintained nor seriously considered maintaining during peacetime a Regular Army of sufficient size to meet the needs of war. The United States has engaged in nine major wars, and ex- tensive reliance has been placed on the citizen-soldier in the first eight of them. That reliance is made clear in the following table.[1] The first column of figures shows the strength of the Regular Army at the beginning of the wars listed; the second column shows the number of Militia, Army National Guard, and Army Reserve troops mobilized for each.

	INITIAL STRENGTH (STANDING)	MOBILIZED (FROM GUARD, ETC)
REVOLUTIONARY WAR	0	250,000
WAR OF 1812	6,744	458,000
MEXICAN WAR	7,365	73,532
SPANISH-AMERICAN WAR	28,183	170,954
WORLD WAR I	127,588	208,000
WORLD WAR II	187,893	377,000
KOREAN WAR	591,487	382,900
VIETNAM WAR	**970,000**	**22,786**

June 7: Resplendent for graduation day, the University of Iowa campus, sprawling along both banks of the Iowa River and climbing to the high bluffs above, wore the best Iowa had to offer: a canopy of hardwoods bursting to fill the sky in new-leaf green, bending shrubs heavy with flowering lilacs and peonies, and green fields so lush that they surely hid leprechauns. The new grads, black gowns billowing and mortarboard tassels swinging, made their way from student housing to the Field House on the opposite bank of the river striding between the porticoes of the Beaux Art classical buildings that adorned the center of campus. Built in the early twentieth century, a quartet of Ionic buildings occupied the four corners of the hill, all designed with symmetry and perfect proportions.

In the center stood the fifth building, Old Cap, built in 1840 in Doric Greek Revival style crowned by a golden dome, the symbol embodied in the University's logo. In 1968 Old Cap housed the office of the President of the University; originally it contained the entire territorial government of Iowa. In Old Cap the legislature authorized the formation of the state's first public university. When the capital moved to Des Moines in 1857, Old Cap became that university. Taken together, the five buildings on the hilltop, the Pentacrest, projected an image with clear meaning: the role of education as idyllic order inherited in the tradition of ancient western civilizations stretching back to the Greeks.

But on April 19, 1865, speakers had eulogized Abraham Lincoln from the steps of Old Cap. And now, nearly 103 years later, those same steps reminded the graduates of the turmoil of Vietnam as that's where the campus war protests were often staged. Ironically, the opposite of idyllic Greek order gripped the campus and the country.

My parents and John's parents joined us in Iowa City for our graduation ceremony and celebration. What should have been an idyllic and forward-looking rite of passage was actually somber as we knew John's draft status officially changed that day. It didn't help that the nation was reeling from the second assassination in two months: in April Martin Luther King, Jr, and now Bobby Kennedy just the day previous.

To me the stately iris all stood at attention, and the wild poppies pushed up anywhere the black loam was disturbed as on fresh graves.

Oh Kareen why do they have a war right now just when we find each other? Kareen we've got more important things than war. Us Kareen you and me in a house. I'll come home at night to you in my house your house our house. We'll have fat happy kids smart kids too. That's more important than a war. Oh Kareen I look at you and you're only nineteen and you're old old like an old woman. Kareen I look at you and I cry inside and I bleed.

—Dalton Trumbo,
Johnny Got His Gun 1939

June 15: Eight days later we married with a sigh of relief from my parents, a bittersweet ceremony as our family and guests knew we would soon be parted. My bouquet of daisies symbolized our innocence. We were together at last, could live together, but for how long? How could our government continue fighting for a cause that a large part of the country didn't believe in? Now returning soldiers held their own demonstrations opposing the war. Some old fuddy-duddies, my parents' friends, who had evidently never been in love, even expressed surprise that we would marry before John went to war rather than waiting to see if he returned. Everyone wondered: How long would we have together? The Bible verse for the ceremony came from Ecclesiastes 3:1–2 used in a protest song "Turn, Turn, Turn" by Pete Seeger: "A time of love, a time of hate, A time of war, a time of peace." At the end Seeger added in his own words a plea for peace.

It is impossible to organize an army solely by coercion. At least some of the commanders and soldiers must truly believe in something, be it God, honour, motherland, manhood or money.
—Yuval Noah Harari, *Sapiens: A Brief History of Humankind 2015*

4

Evicted

August 26, 1968: The Beatles release the single "Revolution" rejecting the violence used by some Vietnam Conflict protesters. It reaches number 12 on the Billboard Hot 100.

August 26–29, 1968: Riots and police brutality mark the Democratic National Convention in Chicago. Young political protesters are arrested; the leaders become known as the Chicago 7. President Johnson's Vice-President, Hubert H Humphrey, wins the Democratic nomination for President.

November 5, 1968: Republican candidate Richard Nixon, promising to end the Vietnam Conflict, is elected President.

December 24, 1968: On Apollo 8, *Frank Borman, Jim Lovell, and Bill Anders become the first humans to orbit the moon. They broadcast this message from space to the largest audience that has ever listened to a human voice: ". . . a Merry Christmas, and God bless all of you-on the good Earth."*

December 31, 1968: US troop levels in Vietnam reach 536,100 Americans, 16,899 die.

January 3, 1969: Senator Edward Kennedy is elected Majority Whip in the US Senate.

January 20, 1969: Richard Nixon is inaugurated 37th President of the US. His speechwriter, William Safire, describes Vietnam as "the bone in the nation's throat."

January 25, 1969: Paris Peace talks begin with representatives from the US, the South Vietnamese government, and North Vietnam's National Liberation Front.

Returning from work one afternoon in late July, I opened the back door into the darkened stairwell leading up to our apartment. Mr. Whitman, our landlord who lived on the main floor, surprised me.

"Pat, do you have a minute?" he croaked, clearing his throat as if he hadn't talked to anyone else all day.

"Sure," I replied noting that his slightly mussed gray hair and rumpled day-old clothing could have been grandfatherly, but the sagging jowls, reminiscent of a bulldog, held few smile lines. He had been a lawyer.

"I was wondering . . . what are your plans for fall?"

"I'll be working, and John is enrolled in grad school . . . the MBA program," I replied.

Then he looked down, not making eye contact. "What's John's draft status?"

Always nervous around him, I gushed, "He's 1-A since graduation, but we're hoping he can make it until fall registration. You know . . . if he can get registered, they'll let him finish the semester before he has to report. With the Presidential election in November, things could change. We're hoping he won't have to go at all."

Raising his rheumy, yet still piercing eyes, he looked directly at me. "Ahh, I see. Well, in that case, we need you to move out by the end of August so we can rent to someone who will definitely be here for the full school year." He had emphasized definitely. "If you leave mid-year . . . you can legally break your lease when John's drafted. We might not be able to rent for second semester."

Before I could gulp, he had retreated back through his door and shut it behind him. I felt devastated. Iowa City contained blocks of stately old homes, Victorians, Queen Annes, Colonial Revivals, mostly white and wooden, set under shady canopies of maples and oaks. After our wedding we moved into one of these, a one-bedroom furnished apartment tucked under the second-floor gambrel roof of a Dutch Revival. We loved our nest. We had been quiet, kept our entrance through the back stairwell swept, and paid the rent before the first of the month.

On the telephone I worked my way through the column of apartment-for-rent want ads, always telling the truth. My strict Methodist upbringing didn't allow lying. With my mother a leader of the church women's group and my father a church Trustee and President of the school board, I grew up feeling watched. They expected me to be the model kid.

Consequently, the apartment calls went something like this: "Hello, I'm calling about your ad in the paper for an apartment to rent."

"The one-bedroom or the two?"

"The one-bedroom furnished. Is that still available?"

"Yes, we just listed it yesterday. Are you renting alone or would you have a roommate?"

"No, it would be for my husband and myself."

"Oh, you're married. And what's his draft status?"

"Uh . . . his draft status? His draft status is 1-A."

"Sorry. We need a rental for the school year, not for a few months. Bye now."

Mr. Whitman wasn't the only landlord in a university town who knew that draftees were protected from any penalty for breaking a lease. However, draftees were not protected from discrimination, nor were they supported by the community they were conscripted to defend.

What were we to do? We needed to live somewhere. Move in with our parents? Both Bettendorf and the farm north of Grinnell were too far away for John to commute to classes. If not a full-time student, he would have no hope of holding on for a semester until after the election. That made the stakes high. We had to live in Iowa City for that to work.

I dialed the number for the last ad, a rental in an apartment complex. The manager answered abruptly. He sounded hurried and papers rustled in the background as he gave me less than his full attention. He was running a business, not renting the other half of his home. That made it easier for me when he asked the big question.

I replied, "My husband is 1-A, but I have a teaching job and will be staying after he's drafted." I lied. It worked. At the end of August, we moved.

One day in early August the mail included a thin envelope from the US Navy. They had not accepted John's application for OCS. It didn't matter. Now that we were married, he had no intention of adding a year's commitment to his time in the military. But now he could be drafted any day. Whenever his notice arrived, he would have to go, unless, of course, it came after he registered for fall semester.

Our lives focused on our mailbox. It clung with others in the shadows under an overhang along the wall near the entrance to our apartment building like bats roosting in a row. John forbade me to pick up the mail. He had to be the one. On work days we often arrived home together, but he sent me in ahead before he would face the damned box. On days off he made hourly treks to check it. As days passed without his so-called Greeting from Uncle Sam, the tension mounted. Would he get it a week before registration? Then, would he get it one of the last few days before registration? And, finally, would he get it the day before?

During this postal waiting game, a week before public school started in Iowa, I interviewed for a teaching job in Wilton, midway between Iowa City and Bettendorf. I had turned down all offers so far and had quit applying because I didn't know where I would be living fall semester. If John was drafted, I needed the support of my family in Bettendorf, but if he made it until fall registration and beyond, I needed to be with him in Iowa City. Wilton was perfect. I could commute from Iowa City or from Bettendorf. I accepted the contract to teach sixth and seventh grade language arts with a verbal assurance that once my husband was drafted, I was out of there the first moment I could join him—with no hard feelings. I now had made half my lie come true. I did have a teaching job, but I still had no desire to stay alone in Iowa City once John left.

Amidst our own personal chaos came the news from the Democratic convention in Chicago, only 200 miles away. We watched on TV the violent confrontation between student anti-war protestors and the Chicago police. Who was responsible? Who was at fault? Were the students inciting riots? Or were the police over-reacting? How had it come to this in the United States of America?

Every morning I left a sleeping John before seven o'clock every morning to meet my carpool, but on a morning in early September, he left the apartment at the same time as I did. Before the mail could arrive, on the first day of registration for the 1968 fall semester, John headed to the line forming outside the University of Iowa Field House. This in spite of the fact that those whose surname began with *P* couldn't register until tomorrow, the second day of registration. At the door John explained his draft status at the check-in desk. He should have been sent home. Instead, he was the first to enter. Indeed, he was the first student to register for classes fall semester of 1968. Before the mail arrived.

That evening, highlighted in the brilliant slant of the late day sun, he waited for me on the front steps of our building. Again, I didn't need words to know what had happened., He was jumping up and down, screaming, pointing to the completed registration in his hand. As I got out of the car, he scooped me up in an enormous bear hug. We whooped and hollered and jigged in circles around the parking lot. We even saluted the mailbox with our middle fingers, but don't tell our parents. John held our ticket to another semester together and the postponement of his induction until after the Presidential election.

It was mid-November when John found his Greeting in the mailbox. At least he did not have to report until February 18th. We would have a new President by then, Richard Nixon. Would we still have a draft and a war?

A newfound cache of notes. . . show that Nixon directed his campaign's efforts to scuttle the peace talks, which he feared could give his opponent, Vice President Hubert H. Humphrey, an edge in the 1968 election. On Oct. 22, 1968, he ordered [White House Chief of Staff] Haldeman to "monkey wrench" the initiative [Johnson's peace efforts].

—John A Farrell,
"Nixon's Vietnam Treachery,"
The New York Times 2016

We spent the last weekend before John's induction in Chicago. It was supposed to be a last fling, but we couldn't find any good spirits to bring along. The bitter winter wind whipping off Lake Michigan didn't help. It was a lousy trip. In 47 years we have lived in 6 countries and traveled in over 50, but we have never been back to Chicago. We had hoped for Carpe Diem, to savor our last moments together, but we failed. No springtime in the park that Valentine's Day.

5

―――――◆

February 18, 1969

I'll never forget that ride. My parents' generation always remembered where they were when the Japanese bombed Pearl Harbor while my generation always remembers John Kennedy's assassination. Now, of course, it's 9/11 that no one can forget. My distress that February day, however, was not a public event shared with the nation, and no one in our family had died—yet. Still, this scene was playing all across the country, family by family, and 16,899 American servicemen did come home in a coffin the previous year alone.

This was the worst day of my life. William drove. Vesta, John's mom, sat grim and expressionless in the front passenger seat. John and I, separated by the center hump, sat in back. It had been foggy at daybreak, masking the fields and neighboring farms from view. The clouds still hung low trapping the damp cold near the barren, frosted ground. Inside the two-tone, green Buick, William blasted the defroster, then a few minutes of heat, then back to the defroster. The heat made poor progress in fighting back the arctic air that chilled us and iced the windows. We four seemed alone, submerged in a hostile, frigid sea.

In spite of the cold, John and I unbuttoned our parkas letting our coat tails fall open across the seat between us. Underneath he surreptitiously sought my hand and held tight. Although no one could question their love and devotion, William and Vesta, being of stern Scottish and Mennonite pioneer heritage, frowned on any public displays of affection. We checked the rearview mirror in front for any sign they suspected this wanton handholding, our wariness in spite of being married for eight months and sleeping in the same bed.

We focused on memorizing each other's face, desperately trying to preserve the image. I gazed at his unruly mop of wavy brown hair and even the small scar under his ear which he jokingly called his "Heidelberg dueling scar," words that would eventually turn out to be prophetic. How would he look next time I saw him? He would have a GI haircut, a buzz, no wayward curl trailing onto his forehead. He would wear a pea-green army uniform, no jeans or Oxford button-downs or V-neck sweaters, the university uniform. There was no conversation, only the defroster blasting.

In all too short a time, we reached Newton, the Jasper County seat. William parked under the leafless, overhanging trees, sentinels of the pioneer past, that guarded the Court House where drafted Jasper County boys reported for induction into the US Army.

I didn't know what would happen now with his parents right there in the front seat. I did not intend to shake hands and send him off to the army. He opened the door and slid out pulling me by the hand. On the curb he gathered me inside his open coat in a tight embrace. We kissed. We looked into each others' eyes and simultaneously whispered, "I love you." So relieved and thankful for this open display of affection, I somehow managed to hold the tears. I would have lots of time for crying, alone, without making it harder for him to leave. Neither of us knew when we would be together again. He turned away, hunched down inside his coat, eyes on the pavement, and strode off under the leaden sky into the gray stone building. I knew he felt sad and lonely, perhaps confused, definitely angry, but mostly afraid. He did not turn back. I understood.

Then there was this freedom the little guys were always getting killed for. Was it freedom from another country? Freedom from work or disease or death? Freedom from your mother-in-law? Please mister give us a bill of sale on this freedom before we go out and get killed. Give us a bill of sale drawn up plainly in advance what we're getting killed for ... so we can be sure after we've won your war that we've got the same kind of freedom we bargained for.

—Dalton Trumbo,
Johnny Got His Gun 1939

I learned that courage was not the absence of fear, but the triumph over it. The brave man is not he who does not feel afraid, but he who conquers that fear.

—Nelson Mandela,
A Long Walk to Freedom:
The Autobiography of Nelson Mandela
1995

BOOK TWO

◆——◆

IN THE ARMY NOW

6

◆———————◆

Heavy Breathing

February 24, 1969: In Tinker v Des Moines Independent Community School District, the US Supreme Court rules for the student protesters suspended for wearing black armbands to school. According to the Court, students do not lose their First Amendment rights when they step onto school property.

March 8, 1969: A Gallup poll reveals that two of three Democrats would choose Senator Edward (Ted) Kennedy, younger brother of the assassinated brothers John and Robert Kennedy, for their next President.

March 1969: Mario Puzo's novel The Godfather, *the epic story of a Sicilian immigrant who becomes the head of a major American crime family, is published.*

March 1969: Kurt Vonnegut's anti-war novel, Slaughterhouse Five, *is published. Vonnegut's main character, a US soldier captured by the Germans in World War II, survives the US fire-bombing of Dresden.*

How would I hear from John? Letter? Phone call? When would it be? I had no idea. Probably by mail, I decided. I guessed a phone call would be a privilege to be earned over time by a new draftee.

Meanwhile, feeling like a zombie, I returned to Wilton. I had broken our lease in Iowa City saying that I had changed my mind about staying there once John reported for duty. Lying still didn't come naturally, but I did it.

John didn't want to worry about me driving on the wintry roads, our carpool had already survived one accident, so I didn't move to my folks in Bettendorf. Instead we moved my clothes into a boarding house in Wilton before John left.

It wasn't the old turn-of-the-century, wooden-frame, two-story with creaking stairs that normally comes to mind, but rather an almost-new, ranch-style home. Linda, the high school home economics teacher, young and single, lived in the house, too. Our bedrooms and the shared hall bath were on the main floor, a blur of pink ruffles in my memory. Mrs. Hall, our landlady, had recently finished the basement, mostly in turquoise, definitely the decorator color for the sixties. With a large recreation room and kitchen, we could cook dinners, watch TV, spread out lesson-plan preparations, or use her sewing machine. On the weekends I alternated driving to my parents or John's parents for the love and support I craved.

Each morning I would head for school early allowing time to stop in the library to read the war news from the front page of the *Des Moines Register*. With the troop involvement in Vietnam continuing to escalate in spite of Nixon's campaign promise of a "secret plan" to end the war, it wasn't good news. Often I found myself dashing into the restroom and locking myself in a stall so that no one would see my tears. When the bell rang, I would blow my nose and dab at my eyes before heading to my classroom.

My students were my saviors. As typical middle-schoolers, they wiggled and giggled and poured their creativity into their class projects. Keeping all of that energy channeled in a positive direction kept my mind occupied and focused for the day. Each class was like uncorking a bottle and letting the genie out to play—while guarding against her running away. We could have great fun with the genie, but I always had to be able to put her back in the bottle if and when I said. So, gratefully my day would pass immersed in my students' problems or hijinks, with no opportunity to think of my own. In the more quiet evenings, however, the Elephant of Fear loomed over my every activity and faithfully climbed right into bed with me each night, keeping me awake with his snoring.

I did hear from John quickly—a postcard—provided by the army at the induction center in Newton and mailed from there. It told me that he was being sent to Fort Polk, Louisiana, known as the epicenter of preparing cannon fodder for Vietnam. I was to let his folks know that the civilian clothes he had on when he reported, including his winter coat, were being shipped to them at the farm where the rest of our household goods were now stored, basically our college textbooks, our wedding presents, and his clothes. Now my fears had a location, Fort Polk, swamps and snakes and gators and bugs! What was happening to him? I knew that basic training intended to tear down the civilian and rebuild a dedicated, unquestioning member of the United States Army. I thought of John as a sensitive, gentle soul, especially loved for his humor, not a tough guy. He was bright and questioning, but *why* would not be allowed in his new vocabulary. How would he bear up? Would he change? How could he manage alone, more specifically, without me?

When the phone rang in the evening, both Mrs. Hall and Linda stayed clear letting me jump for it. Perhaps 10 days after John had left, I pounced on the ringing thing saying my cheeriest "Hello," but I could only hear heavy breathing, a croupy, rasping sound. Then silence.

Finally, a husky voice became barely audible, "Pat, honey? Can't you even recognize your husband?"

"John, John? Is that you?" Only one person called me "honey." "What's wrong? John?"

"I have pneumonia," he wheezed. "I'm in the hospital." The rest was unintelligible.

"What? What hospital? Where? I can't hear you?" Then I heard a tight, racking cough that went on and on, so painful that knowing it came from John made the tiny hairs on my neck rise.

"I can't stand up any longer. I love you." Click.

That was it. I had no way to call him back, no one else to call about him. I didn't know where he was really, in a civilian or military hospital. I had no idea how serious his illness was. With antibiotics most people, especially young people, recovered from pneumonia, but not everyone. I knew that during the Civil War, more soldiers died from disease than from combat injuries, including one of my own great-grandfathers. Hopefully, the Army had advanced their hygiene practices. I could do nothing but go on with life and hope for another call, soon!

The next call and the next were not terribly different. At the base hospital he had to stand in a long line to use the pay phone, and by the time it was his turn, he fought to stay on his feet, too weak to talk. He would cough uncontrollably wheezing out the command for me to do the talking.

So, the back story, one I never heard until after he left the hospital: On the tarmac his chartered flight from Des

Moines to Fort Polk, Louisiana, was diverted to Fort Lewis, Washington. Fort Polk had shut down due to a spinal meningitis epidemic. Instead John and the other new Iowa inductees were sent to Fort Lewis in February with nothing but basic cotton army-issue fatigues. They may have had dental fillings or a weddings ring, but not another thing. In spite of the cold Iowa weather, coats hadn't been issued for transit to Fort Polk.

They arrived in Washington around midnight. From the airport a bus took them to Fort Lewis, dumped them, and told them to stand outside where they could be seen. Someone in charge should arrive soon. But no one ever came. They huddled together beneath the eaves like green penguins, hopping from one foot to another, trying as a group to preserve their warmth and protect themselves from the winter rain which fell steadily all night.

Just before dawn a kitchen worker came by on his way to breakfast duty, just an enlisted grunt, a potato-peeler. "What the *@#* are you guys doin' out here?"

John has always remembered this guy. Like the bus driver, he could have taken the army approach: "It's not my job, so I'm not messin' with it." But he took the humanitarian view and made a phone call. They were rescued, but five hours overnight in freezing winter rain took its toll. A week or so later, after fighting his illness with no sympathy from his sergeant, he passed out and was taken away by ambulance. Soon the Upper Respiratory Unit of the hospital held a dozen or more Iowa boys from that plane. Following three weeks of hospitalization, he was released and sent back to his basic training unit, but he had missed too much to continue with that platoon and had to await reassignment. Four weeks in the army and only starting basic training—again! Four weeks apart for nothing! Although catastrophic at the time, ironically, this delay possibly saved John from the infantry.

> They carried all of the emotional baggage of men who might die. . . . They carried the common secret of cowardice barely restrained, the instinct to run or freeze or hide, and in many respects this was the hardest burden of all, for it could never be put down, it required perfect balance and perfect posture. They carried their reputations. They carried the soldier's greatest fear, which was the fear of blushing. Men killed and died, because they were embarrassed not to. . . . They died so as not to die of embarrassment.
>
> —Tim O'Brien,
> *The Things They Carried* 1990

Missing Pat
The first of 10 cartoons that John sent home in letters to
Pat or to their parents during his time in the army.

7

The Smell of the Ground

On April 1 the ringing phone awakened me. First light barely separated the leafless trees from the horizon out my window. The phone never rang at this hour.

Then Mrs. Hall called, "Pat, it's for you." My heart flipped. The rare calls from John came in the evening. Had something happened to him again? I ran for the phone. It was Mom. She was choking back tears. "Patty, my mother has passed away."

I would not be honest if I did not confess to a slight relief, but still it was not good news. I loved my Grandma Black. She was 84, bedridden, blind, and in a nursing home, so it was not unexpected, perhaps not without its mercies, but still—too final.

During my childhood my family travelled to visit both of my Grandma's in northeastern Kansas every Easter and every Thanksgiving during school vacations. I remembered the house of my maternal grandmother, Grandma Black, as high adventure. Fires had to be built in the wood stoves each morning. Each evening Grandma laid magazines on the parlor-stove warming tray before transferring them to our beds. I equated bedtime with the roasting smell of hot newsprint. Their warmth eased the shock of cold flesh meeting sheets in a bedroom without central heat. The "facilities" were out the back door and down the path and came with spider webs and bugs that, unlike me, didn't mind the odor. At night there was the chamber pot under the bed, steam rising from the hot contents meeting the cold porcelain, until a cloth was thrown over the top to lessen the stench. At her house I seldom succumbed to any bathroom urges in the middle of the night. Washing was done from water hand-pumped at the kitchen sink and heated on the stove.

Yet, in spite of baking over a hand-built fire in the kitchen stove, Grandma Black's cinnamon rolls, made from scratch, melted in the mouth, light enough to float you to heaven. And every visit started with a greeting that included a bowl of her homemade chocolate pudding made especially for me, undisputedly the origin of my "chocoholism."

The next day I arranged for a sub so I could accompany my parents to Kansas for Grandma's funeral. Before making her funeral arrangements, we first visited my father's mother, Grandma Veach, age 85 and also in a nursing home. I remember my shock. To me the frail old lady in the wheel chair with the short and choppy uncombed hair hardly resembled the grandma I remembered. I hadn't seen either of my grandmas since before college. Neither had been well enough to travel to my wedding. We could only spend a few minutes with Grandma Veach as we had funeral arrangements to make for Grandma Black.

The next morning, at my aunt's house, the phone rang yet again before the break of dawn. My mother quickly appeared at my bedside. "Patty, Patty. Wake up. You have to get up quickly. It's Grandma Veach. That phone call was from her nursing home. She's in a coma. We need to leave now!" So very early on the morning we had meant to spend with Grandma Veach, we arrived to be at her bedside as she died. An ulcer perforated during the night, and she was bleeding to death. As we entered, the nurse pulled away the fabric screen surrounding her bed. She laid unconscious, her head nestled in a pillow, with the bed slightly elevated so we could easily see her face, ashen but serene. Her few remaining breaths came so far apart. Each time, after such a long pause, I thought there couldn't possibly be another one, but for an hour or so, they kept coming. Finally, no more. The nurse took her pulse and announced she was gone.

I'll never forget my father's despairing cry, "Mommy!" Wiping away tears, we took turns lightly kissing her still-warm forehead.

I also cherished my memories of visits to Grandma Veach's house, always on the same twice-annual trips to Kansas. In the small town of Hutton, I was trusted to walk downtown by myself, two blocks to the left and two blocks to the right, with pennies from Grandma in my pocket to spend however I wanted. I slept in her bed, the two of us together. I especially remember her beginning and ending each day seated at her dressing table at the foot of the bed. I helped her brush her silver hair that, once unbraided, hung to below her waist. It was magnificent, and I marveled at how she braided it each morning and coiled the braids around her head like a crown. She was the queen, and I was her princess. Both of my grandmothers had loved me and delighted in my every accomplishment as only grandmothers can!

On April 4, 1969, Grandma Black's funeral took place at the Mercer Funeral Home in Hutton, Kansas, with her burial immediately following in Dryver, a few miles away, where she had lived most of her life. The next day Grandma Veach's service was held in the same funeral home but with burial following in the Hutton Cemetery. Of course, we all regretted not spending more time with Grandma Veach the first day, but even more I have always regretted, and especially now that I have become a grandma myself, that it had not seemed urgent to John and me, in the selfishness and distraction of youth, to take time from our jobs and schooling to make a trip, a day's drive each way, to introduce him to my grandmothers. They never knew him.

I grieved for my grandmothers, for their adoring love, and for my lost childhood. I struggled with the fact that death is part of life; generally, granddaughters do outlive grandmothers. Now as a Grandma myself, I realize I represented their spark of immortality. I had Grandma Veach's big brown eyes and Grandma Black's right ear that stuck out through any hairdo. How many hours of my youth had I spent rearranging my hair to cover it? But now it makes me smile as it reminds me of her and her chocolate pudding.

But the worst of those funereal days, no matter how hard I fought to turn it off, was the slide show running inside my head. I saw a backdrop mirroring eastern Kansas, much like Iowa: a cemetery on a gray, not-yet-spring day, with still-brown grass, spongy from overnight rain. My cheeks stung and my eyes watered from the brisk wind across the prairie. I turned to walk away from an imagined gravesite but looked back over my shoulder just as the gravediggers began to lower a flag-draped casket, a soldier, into the cold ground. If that came to pass, I didn't know how I would survive.

There will come soft rains
and the smell of the ground,
And swallows calling with their shimmering sound;
And frogs in the pools singing at night,
And wild-plum trees in tremulous white;
Robins will wear their feathery fire
Whistling their whims on a low fence-wire
And not one will know of the war, not one
Will care at last when it is done.
Not one would mind, neither bird nor tree,
If mankind perished utterly;
And Spring herself, when she woke at dawn,
Would scarcely know that we were gone.
—Sara Teasdale, "There Will Come
Soft Rains" 1918

8

It's a Mountain

April 1969: US combat deaths surpass 33,629, the total number in the Korean War.

April 9–10, 1969: Student war protestors take over the administrative center at Harvard University. After riot police charge the building taking 196 students to jail, Harvard students declare a strike and rally with over 10,000 students participating.

April 10, 1969: Secretary of Defense Melvin Laird is ordered to prepare a timetable for what will become known as Vietnamization, *the progressive transfer of the war effort to the South Vietnamese military leaving American personnel to serve only in support and advisory roles for a limited period of time.*

April 19–23, 1969: Vietnam veterans march in Washington, DC, to protest the war they themselves fought in. They lobby their Congressmen and lay wreaths on graves in Arlington National Cemetery. They end the protest by throwing combat ribbons, helmets, uniforms, and toy weapons on the Capitol steps.

April 30, 1969: US troop strength in Vietnam reaches 543,482, the peak of US troop involvement during the conflict.

This chapter is John's experience, not mine. I could only worry while he lived through it, so I write from the stories he has shared with me. The M14 rifle became his new life partner. In training a recruit carries it everywhere, learns to take it apart, clean and reassemble it, in a hurry, over and over again. Everyday life started at 04:30, that's military time for four-thirty in the morning. It included lots of running, push-ups, sit-ups, and obstacle courses and didn't include decent food or free time. He had experiences he would rather have skipped in life like learning to throw live grenades or crawling on knees and elbows under live machine-gun fire with his M14 cradled in his arms. He had fire duty in the middle of the night and used latrines with no stalls, just sit to do your thing right in front of everybody. A private has no privacy. Always the sergeants told the trainees what to do, when to do it, and how to do it, usually yelling.

While most trainees complained about the forced marches with full pack, being from the midwestern flatlands, John actually waxed eloquent about the "walks" through the misty, pine-scented forests of Washington state. He often described the first time the new recruits spied Mt. Rainier:

"What's that?" a recruit asked pointing to the horizon.

"Some weird clouds," someone else responded.

And then a chorus from the platoon: "Oh, my god! It's a mountain."

Rainier, when visible rising through its mantle of clouds, dominated at that close distance. To him that imposing peak represented freedom and escape. Its majesty, serenity, and power provided an allure, an emotional refuge into another world.

We have since lived in the foothills of the Rockies, the Sierras, and the Himalayas, all with towering peaks and awe-inspiring vistas for sure. And now in retirement, we see Pike's Peak as we drive into our neighborhood, but nowhere has a single peak loomed over the frightening world of mankind like Rainier did for John in basic training. This dramatic first experience started his love affair with the mountains that has enriched and shaped our lives in Colorado as hikers, campers, backpackers, skiers, and snowshoers. At age 69 John's biggest thrill is being at our family townhome at the base of Keystone Mountain with our kids and their families so that he can ski with his grandkids, all five of them. To be sure they humor him. Taking a run with Grandpa means stopping at the bottom to wait for Grandpa, even the five-year old is way ahead. For our sons, life is a mountain, and now for our grandsons and granddaughter, too.

The rifle is the Infantryman's basic weapon. It gives him an individual and powerful capability for combat. To benefit the most from this capability, the infantryman must develop two skills to an equal degree: he must be able to fire his weapon well enough to get hits on battlefield targets, and he must know enough about its working parts to keep it operating.
—Field Manual No. 23-8, Department of the Army 1965

In his first platoon, before pneumonia, the other draftees, just like John, had received their Greeting from Uncle Sam during the fall semester of grad school. The Selective Service allowed them to finish the semester, and, consequently, all reported for induction at about the same time. With one semester toward an MBA, John was among the least educated. Most were PhD candidates; they came from various disciplines, anthropology through zoology, only doctors and dentists were still exempt. So, it depended on how you looked at it: no longer could the rich grad school boys escape the draft versus the nation was using it's brightest as cannon fodder.

In John's next platoon, many of the recruits came from California, did not have college experience, and held a variety of blue-collar jobs, yet to John they seemed more cosmopolitan than an Iowa farm boy. Even without much in common, they all bonded with their single goal: to get the hell out of here. They looked out for each other however they could, no cliques, no bullying. So, as the time approached for the final written test, which had to be passed to get out of basic training, John sensed the fear of one of the congenial guys, a strong, handsome fellow, but illiterate. Since John usually finished any test first, the sergeant requested that John read the test aloud to this fellow.

In a hushed voice, so as not to disturb the others still testing, John read, "Question 1: What is the effective firing range of an M14 rifle? Answer A: 150 feet; Answer B: 300 feet; Answer C *(John read slowly and a bit louder to indicate it was the correct answer.)* 500 feet; Answer D: 750 feet." Nearly 47 years later, he still treasures the grateful smile when his pal realized what John was doing for him.

> Want to know what it's like to be in the Army? Try standing in one place, ramrod straight and perfectly still. If a mosquito bites you, don't slap it. If sweat rolls into your eye, don't wipe it away. And if you scratch your thigh, do 20 push-ups and jump back into position.
>
> —Frank Pellegrini, *Time,* from "He's in the Army Now. Well, Almost . . ." 1999

After passing all the tests at the end of basic training, John, like the other trainees, received orders for his Advanced Individual Training. Of course, infantry and artillery were most feared, but John drew the military police. Since that specialty required higher qualifications, including higher test results on the army's equivalent to the IQ test, we have always thought that finishing basic training without PhD candidates dominating the platoon, might have made John the more likely plum for this job. Although not infantry "grunts," the MPs did provide battlefield support in the combat zones of Vietnam securing the area, especially the roads and bridges needed for the circulation of men and materiel. The army sent him to Fort Gordon in Augusta, Georgia, for military police training. He soon discovered that he would be eligible for 36-hour weekend passes.

By this time I was finishing the school year. It had taken John almost an entire semester to get through what was supposed to be eight weeks of basic training. Indeed, his first pass came through for Memorial Day weekend. In less than a week I had found another boarding house, now in Augusta, Georgia, packed my bags, averaged my grades, cleaned out my classroom, and taken John's Fairlane 500 for an oil change. Literally, I was ready to roll. My school made good on their promise to let me go whenever I could join John. As it turned out, I left with only one day remaining in my contract, an inservice day without student contact on the Tuesday following Memorial Day.

My parents, although uneasy about me driving alone from Iowa to Georgia, knew they couldn't stop me, so my mother declared she was coming along and to seal the deal bought herself a plane ticket home from Georgia. My dad, remember, had volunteered during World War II after they were married, and they had faced separation during basic training themselves before he received a medical discharge. I was glad for her company, but with glaucoma and macular degeneration, she could neither help with the driving nor the map reading. For that part I was on my own having never driven farther than 90 miles from Wilton west to John's parents. I had never negotiated the tangled spaghetti of intersecting interstate highways, such as existed in Atlanta. Mom was brave. And I was on my way!

9

◆━━━━◆

Swamps, Snakes, Gators, and Bugs

June 8, 1969: Nixon begins to withdraw forces from Vietnam by meeting with South Vietnam's President Nguyen Van Thieu on Midway Island to announce the first increment of redeployment.

June 27, 1969: In an article titled "The Faces of the American Dead in Vietnam: One Week's Toll," Life magazine prints the portraits of the 242 Americans killed in action in Vietnam during a single week in June, a week identified by the magazine as "average for any seven-day period during the war." Twelve pages feature the faces of young people, mostly working-class black and white men, some in uniform, some posing for high-school graduation in cap and gown.

After two long days of driving, Mom and I passed through the front gate of Fort Gordon in Augusta, Georgia, on Sunday, May 25. Pine and cypress trees dominated the landscape, the canopy above giving way to various palms and palmettos sticking from the twisted vines underneath, wherever natural growth was allowed. Across the entrance road lay a snake, as long as the road was wide: road kill. The swamps and snakes and gators and bugs that I had pictured at Fort Polk, Louisiana, all thrived here, and John would live among them as he went on maneuvers bivouacking at night. All four species of poisonous snakes indigenous to the United States lurked

73

in the swamps of Fort Gordon: eastern cottonmouths, rattlesnakes, water moccasins, and southern copperheads. Although still May, under the full sun of mid-afternoon, the temperature soared into the nineties, an exact match for the humidity, also in the nineties. Without air conditioning in the car, I felt my coiffured Mary-Tyler-Moore flip fall limp as moisture seeped from my every pore. How attractive!

As we passed offices, classrooms, and row after row of rectangular, box-shaped barracks, troops in formation appeared around each corner chanting various versions of marching "cadences," a form of call and response between the trainees and their drill sergeant, shouted as they marched from one training activity to another. I couldn't believe what I was hearing!

Troops:	If I die in Vietnam, Send my body home to mom. Fold my hands across my chest. Tell my girl I done my best.
Drill Sergeant:	Sound-off
Troops:	1 - 2
Drill Sergeant:	Sound-off
Troops:	3 - 4
Drill Sergeant:	Cadence count
Troops:	1 - 2 - 3 - 4 1 - 2 (skip two beats) 3 - 4 (yell louder)

We found John's barracks, and, in spite of his buzzed, GI haircut, I recognized him waiting at the curb. I threw the car into park, threw open the door, and threw myself into his arms. We kissed and pulled back to look at each other and kissed and looked and kissed and looked. Too good to be true!

He was even thrilled to see his mother-in-law! After a kiss on the cheek for her, too, he threw his duffle through the open back window into his precious Fairlane 500, slid behind the steering wheel, and drove his own car for the first time since mid-February. We had reservations at a nearby motel, two rooms. Much to our amazement, Mom developed a sudden urge to go shopping in the commercial strip across the street leaving us to ourselves until dinner. She, undoubtedly, remembered her first reunion with Dad after his basic training. At least he was home for good.

The next day we dumped my meager belongings at my boarding house. This one did fit the image of a boarding house, especially in the South. It was rambling and gracious, a wooden, three-story home with a sweeping porch across two sides. But the peeling white paint hung from bare patches of wood, that grand porch sagged, and the spacious corner lot, shaded by pines and tupelos, overgrown with palmettos and tangled vines, held barely a blade of grass. In a few more years, it would make a great haunted house only needing a few gravestones engraved with RIP. It was summer in Georgia, but the house was not air conditioned. I was grateful that my room was downstairs in the back so I could keep the windows and curtains wide open and the ceiling fan cranking constantly. Once we unloaded my clothes onto the bed and piled my books on a dresser, we raced for the airport for Mom's flight and then straight to the barracks before John's pass expired.

⁜

I spent my first week applying at temp agencies. I could type and operate an adding machine, so I did get a few days of work during my six weeks in Augusta. The extra money made it possible for us to enjoy John's 36-hour weekend passes. For starters we stayed in air-conditioned motel rooms, rather than my musty bedroom just off the kitchen, where Mrs. Southard and her boarders congregated.

Two weekends later we drove to Atlanta to Six Flags Over Georgia, our first visit ever to an amusement park. In Iowa we had known only carnies and the state fair. We loved the log ride, in 100-degree weather splashing felt great. And the roller coaster, besides creating a breeze, provided an excuse to hold on to each other tight. We screamed with glee! Whoever knew we would be together on our first anniversary?

We had planned when we needed to leave from the farthest end of the park to make it back to Fort Gordon before John's pass expired. With perfect timing one of Georgia's drenching tropical deluges opened up on us at that exact time. It rained cats and dogs, gerbils and parakeets, goats and pot-bellied pigs! Everyone else ducked inside shops and restaurants, or under any overhang, but we had no choice. We had to leave. John would be AWOL. Try telling the drill sergeant you didn't get back in time because it rained.

At first we ran, but within the first minute, the rain soaked us through to our underwear. Running accomplished nothing. We had to walk the length of the park, wait for a tram to shuttle us to the parking lot, and find our car. Once there we pulled our dirty clothes out of the suitcase in the trunk and laid them over the seats to protect the fabric. John pulled into the first service station so we could try to clean up and dry off in the restroom. I remember wringing water out of my underwear, then realizing that I would dry faster without that additional wet layer under my already soaking blouse and shorts. And so, I borrowed from John's Scottish ancestors and adopted the "regimental" tradition for the nearly 150-mile drive back to Fort Gordon. Perhaps a more memorable first anniversary than we had imagined. Of the 47 we've had, we certainly do remember that one best. A whole lot of Carpe Diem, wet Carpe Diem!

Each evening I could look forward to hearing John's voice over the phone. One such evening, a week or so before he was to finish his training at Fort Gordon, the phone rang just after dinner, his usual time. I grabbed for it.

"Hello, Mrs. Southard's Boarding House."

"Hi, honey. It's me."

"Oh, John. So, what was today like?"

"Unbelievable, we had judo lessons. It's quite a kick to throw somebody when they're totally unsuspecting. To pass we had to throw the sergeant—most fun I've had in the army."

We continued sharing our day, nothing very intimate, as he always had a guy behind him in line waiting to call his own mother or sweetheart, and I often had other boarders cleaning up their dinner mess near the phone in the kitchen. At least today there had been nothing about the swamps, spiders, gators, and bugs that prepared him for Vietnam.

"Hey, by the way, before I go, I got orders today for Germany. Love you. Bye."

"What? What did you say?" He had hung up.

Did he say orders for Germany? Was he joking? No, he wouldn't joke about something like that! Did I hear it right? Germany? Not Vietnam? Really? I spent 24 hours without sleep waiting for his next call. Indeed, the next night he confirmed his orders for Germany. I had spent the summer in Europe two years before, just before our engagement, missing John the whole time. Might we enjoy it together: castles, beer halls, wine fests, and cathedrals? But would I be able to go? I knew the army didn't sponsor wives of men under the rank of sergeant. It would be up to us at our own expense, if possible at all. *If possible at all!* He knew nothing one way or the other about that prospect. But Germany was not Vietnam, no swamps, no Viet Cong, we knew that! Only due to such good news, could I overlook him dropping it on me and hanging up, his idea of a joke. I didn't laugh. I was furious at him! This was so out of character! That's the behavior of an insensitive clod. What was he thinking? A universal characteristic resides in all of us human beings: imperfection. He wasn't perfect and neither was I. Marriage did require work, but I have yet to forgive him for that one. Definitely not!

10

A Giant Leap

July 7, 1969: John Lennon releases the single "Give Peace a Chance" written by himself and his new bride Yoko Ono. Tommy Smothers accompanies Lennon on the acoustic guitar. The song reaches #14 on the Billboard Hot 100.

July 14, 1969: The film Easy Rider *starring Peter Fonda, Dennis Hopper and Jack Nicholson is released in the US. The story centers on two hippies traveling on motorcycles from Los Angeles to New Orleans witnessing the contrast of intolerance versus the counterculture.*

July 18, 1969: Senator Edward Kennedy drives his car off a one-lane bridge on Chappaquiddick Island, Massachusetts. While he is able to swim to safety, his young companion Mary Jo Kopechne drowns. Kennedy pleads guilty to a charge of leaving the scene of a crash after causing injury and later receives a two-month suspended jail sentence. The scandalous incident will ruin his chance to run for President.

July 20, 1969: Apollo 11 lands a lunar module on the moon.

July 21, 1969: Neil Armstrong steps out onto the surface of the moon.

July 24, 1969: Apollo 11 returns safely to Earth with its crew.

John yelled over the noisy engine, "No, Pat. Not like that. You have to ease up on the clutch while giving it a little gas,"

"But I can't. I can't get the timing!" I shouted back as the pick-up jerked, coming to rest in an unseen hole.

"You just have to get the feel of it. Put the clutch in and see if you can get us out of here," he snarled bracing himself with one hand on the door handle and the other on the dashboard.

I stomped on the clutch pedal, yanked the gear shift toward me and down, and hit the gas. It was too much. We lurched forward, and the truck died, pitching us toward the windshield. Why couldn't I get it?

Noticing the tears escaping down my cheeks, he sighed as he said, "I think that's enough for today. We can try again tomorrow."

We were back on the farm in Iowa. Just after the Fourth of July, with a peck of Georgia peaches for each set of parents, we had pointed the Fairlane 500 north. John had three weeks of leave before they would send him to Germany. Although I could not officially accompany him, I had been to Germany before, and I knew I could get myself back there. They couldn't keep me from living in the town where he was stationed, could they? Yet the military discouraged such arrangements, so it could also mean a year and a half of separation. Still, it was not Vietnam! We had hope! To be prepared, since European cars still had manual transmissions, I needed to learn to drive a stick shift, so we spent hours in the pasture as I tried to maneuver his dad's rusty 1953 International pickup through the tall grass while dodging cow pies.

As you have known since Chapter 1, John has been my editor. After reading the dialogue above, he suggested this alternate version:

"That's all right, sweetie," John said soothingly displaying his patience and equanimity.

"But I can't. I can't get the timing," I whined.

"You're doing great. You've just about got it," he purred.

On the night of July 21, 1969, John's niece and nephew happened to be staying with their Grandma Vesta and Grandpa William for the night. Grandma Vesta, a retired kindergarten teacher, made staying at her house a special event for her grandchildren, two-year old Andy and seven-year old Roseann. Grandma kept all of her teaching props, from Native American dolls to space vehicles, set up in a play room in the attic. The highlight, all children agreed, was a home-made, silver rocket from her space unit. With a window and a door, it stood tall enough and wide enough to climb inside. So, of course, Grandma allowed the children to stay up late on this special evening to watch space-exploration history in the making. We all gathered in front of the TV crammed into the small upstairs apartment living room, four generations, seated on the sagging couch, on the hardwood floor, and on stiff-backed chairs brought in from the dining room, to watch Neil Armstrong emerge from the lunar landing module onto the surface of the moon. Together we heard his historic words: "That's one small step for man, one giant leap for mankind."

The next morning under a brilliant blue summer sky, Grandpa Burton went out early to tend his beloved rose garden, before the heat of the day. He kneeled on his ancient canvas cushion, perhaps once khaki-colored, but now nearly black from the rich Iowa earth of many such gardening sessions. His gloved hands tenderly worked with the soft fragrant blossoms and prickly branches as he pruned and trimmed wherever needed. Then quietly, mid-morning, he rolled over on his side and died with a rose in his hand. Born in 1879 he had started life in the horse and buggy age, without electricity or a telephone. On his last day alive, he had witnessed in real time, through the miracle of television, a man walking on the moon.

Thankfully, we were together for this funeral, and I learned much about John's family's pioneer background, a heritage that defined them. Grandpa's parents had migrated by wagon train to Iowa immediately after the Civil War. They had broken prairie with a team of oxen, a hard life, but they had prospered. Grandpa was the first generation born in the new pioneer home, and he married a neighbor girl, also of the first generation of her family born in Iowa.

Grandpa's service took place under the spire of the white wooden-frame Newburg Congregational Church where John had been confirmed. A bronze plaque in the churchyard named the church's Christian pioneer founders including Grandpa's mother- and father-in-law. His burial followed several miles away in Hickory Grove Cemetery, high on a heavily timbered hill, with views back across the green fields to the church and town. The cemetery occupied land donated in 1872 by his maternal grandparents for "a church house and public burying ground." The marker stones in this cemetery make a 3-D family tree for John's family, and some day, our ashes will lie among them.

Soon after Grandpa's service, it was time to say good-bye to each other yet again. We had no idea how long we would be apart, a few weeks or the remainder of John's hitch. Yes, there was unknown, but it did not include swamps and snakes and gators and bugs. Or Viet Cong!

11

◆————————◆

07:00 or 19:00?

August 12, 1969: US soldiers mutiny during battle in the Song Chang Valley in South Vietnam.

August 15–18, 1969: The Woodstock Music and Art Festival, *billed as "Three Days of Peace and Love," is held on a farm near Bethel, New York, and attracts 300,000-500,000 (sources vary) counterculture enthusiasts. It becomes the iconic rock event of the 20th century.*

August 20, 1969: Arlo Guthrie's film Alice's Restaurant *premiers. The movie presents an adaptation of Guthrie's narrative song about being rejected as unfit for the draft due to his arrest for littering.*

Counting the hours until I thought I would see John, I boarded the Icelandic flight just before midnight as I had done two years previously when I spent the summer traveling in Europe. As the plane gathered speed on the runway, just as I expected to feel the liftoff, the pilot slammed on the brakes, hard! Pitched against the seat back in front of me, I rebounded and turned to peer out the window into the darkness. In front of the plane, lights from buildings at the end of the runway grew larger and larger coming straight at us. People across the aisle who could see the engines on that side yelled, "Smoke. Smoke. There's smoke coming from the engine." Minutes before, as I had boarded the flight, I had been counting the hours

84

until I would see John. Now, panicked, I wondered: "Would I see John at all?" Thus began my trip to Germany.

Here's what happened in August that made that trip possible. Once the Army assigned John to the 537th MP Company in Mannheim, Germany, he immediately found out that a couple of enlisted guys had wives in-country that did not live in the barracks. These couples rented apartments "on the economy." That meant they rented from Germans with rent paid in Deutschmarks, not US dollars. Married housing was not provided by the Army for anyone below the rank of sergeant. One of these enlisted couples was leaving at the end of August, so John arranged to rent their apartment beginning September 1. We would be able to buy food and some household goods at the Commissary and PX and to receive health services on base, but, excepting John's meager PFC paycheck, that was all the support we would get from the army. We never considered our financial situation. We never ran the numbers to see if we could manage rent, groceries, car maintenance, and so on. Actually, we had no idea how much any of those things would cost in Germany.

I immediately got my ticket on Icelandic, now known as Icelandair, the cheapest commercial fare to Europe in 1969 as they still flew prop-jet planes and stopped in Reykjavik to refuel with service to only one destination on the continent, Luxembourg. There, I could get a bus to Mannheim.

I spent most of August filling out forms hoping I could work in Germany because we did fear his pay might not cover the rent and the groceries. I ordered transcripts, copied recommendations, and even got fingerprinted, in order to apply for a teaching position in the Department of Defense Dependents Schools for the sons and daughters of military personnel stationed in Germany. I knew the school year would already be underway, so for back-up I took the Civil Service exam and typing test required for a secretarial job with the Army. Ten years of piano lessons translated into good results on speed-typing tests, and the multiple-choice test hardly wrinkled my brow after the Graduate Record Exam for grad school entrance that I had taken the year before. I had confidence that I would be able to support us. What if I couldn't get a job? We never even thought about it.

Ignoring the realities, I packed my winter clothes, a few small kitchen appliances and some towels in small boxes that could be shipped to servicemen overseas. Those going by boat would take 6-8 weeks to arrive, so I splurged on a few necessities sending them by air, an extravagance in our financial situation. William helped me sell the beloved white-and-turquoise Fairlane 500 which I almost thought of as an extension of John, but we needed the proceeds to buy a car in Germany. By the last day of August, I was ready to fly!

In 1969 flying provided an elite form of transportation. I dressed to the nines, a new tailored red and gold paisley sheath dress with solid gold tunic-length vest that I had made while John was in Basic Training, plus nylons and heels, of course. Today, I fly in the closest thing to pajamas that I can wear in public. Mom, Dad, and my little brother, Mike, all took me to the airport in Moline, Illinois, where I could catch a flight to JFK for my Icelandic connection. We had taken Dad to the airport a few times to fly to his company's home office in Newark. It was a big deal, and each time we went as a family. He always stopped at the automated kiosk for trip insurance before boarding. We passed that kiosk, too, but I wasn't a breadwinner, so my loss wouldn't leave the family destitute. While the insurance wasn't necessary for me, it did cause images of planes dropping into bodies of water to cross my mind. Who knew why planes could fly? That hadn't been in the curriculum in high school physics in 1963.

My family bid me the proverbial tearful farewell. Because of the difficulty and expense of transatlantic telephone communication at that time, they knew they would have to wait for a letter from Mannheim to know that I had arrived safely. How long would that take? They did not expect to hear my voice again for a year and a half. Their daughter had left for Europe before, but on a student tour. The tour company arranged the transportation, hotels, and meals, and a guide took care of all of the day-to-day details. All I had had to do was pack my bag, pay my money earned from summer jobs, and show up.

But now, I was on my own until I found John. Even together, we were just two kids alone in a foreign country trying to stay together on an army PFC's pay. In the late sixties, Europe was practically terra incognito for Iowans. John's parents had never been out of the country; my parents had been to Canada. When I went to Europe that first time, I had only known one other person who had been there, Mrs. Rosecrans, one of my high school English teachers. Now I intended not only to travel in Europe, but to live there. Mom couldn't come along for the drive like she did to Fort Gordon. From the love and protection of my secure childhood home, I was taking my own "giant leap." I had already taken my small step, getting married.

Now, I was leaving for Germany to make a new home with my husband. I was just going! Alone, I had found my way late at night through the confusing signs and jams of strangers at JFK and plopped into my seat aboard the Icelandic plane just at midnight.

What gives value to travel is fear. It is the fact that, at a certain moment, when we are so far from our own country . . . we are seized by a vague fear, and an instinctive desire to go back to the protection of old habits . . . this is why we should not say that we travel for pleasure. There is no pleasure in traveling, and I look upon it more as an occasion for spiritual testing . . . .
—Albert Camus, *Notebooks* 1935

After the aborted takeoff, the plane did stop before hitting the buildings, the smoke did not become fire, and the plane taxied back to the terminal where we deplaned, uninjured but rattled. An hour later the mechanical difficulty, supposedly fixed, Icelandic reloaded the plane. I wondered with dread: did they really fix the unnamed problem or would it cause trouble over the ocean? As I climbed up the stairs into the plane, the acrid smell of oil and jet fuel from the tarmac made my sinuses ache and my stomach pitch. This time we sat on the tarmac for over an hour on a scorching, sticky August night, no air conditioning, no restrooms, no water, and then deplaned again, my worst fears confirmed. We waited some more. Now it's the middle of the night. No one has faith in Icelandic. Some passengers are leaving, probably people who lived in New York. Again, Icelandic called for boarding. I didn't want to get back on, but what could I do? Fly home to Mom and Dad, not see John for a year and a half? After another wait on the tarmac, we deplaned for the third time.

Now it's 4:00 am. The PA announced that buses were coming to take us to a hotel for the rest of the night. We waited for over an hour, for the buses had to come from Manhattan. It took another hour for them to return with us to the hotel, also in Manhattan. At six-thirty in the morning, the hotel had one clerk on duty to check in some 200 passengers, mostly wanting separate rooms. Waiting in that line, my head swirled in one direction and my stomach in the other. As I signed the register, I didn't know if I was going to pass out or throw up.

When the clerk finally pushed my key at me, I heard an announcement: "All Icelandic passengers should assemble in the lobby for return to the airport at eight o'clock." It was now seven-thirty. Too exhausted to react, I robotically entered the elevator, found my room, put my key in one way and then another before unlocking the door, but my mind screamed: "Eight o'clock? Why bother with a hotel room for a half hour?" I didn't dare lie down. What if I fell asleep and missed the bus? I knew the desk clerk couldn't handle 200 wake up calls. I didn't even have a much-needed toothbrush.

So, back in the lobby at eight o'clock, there were no buses for pick-up; however, we were given vouchers for breakfast, but warned not to linger in case the buses arrived. Not until two o'clock in the afternoon did they return. Dazed and disheveled, I climbed the steps into the bus and found a seat, but they were not going to the airport. They took us to a restaurant for lunch in the middle of the afternoon. Finally, the bus deposited us at JFK. We boarded the plane and ultimately took off at five o'clock, 17 hours behind schedule. I had no way to communicate with John. What would he think when I didn't show up? He didn't know exactly when I would get to Mannheim, but after an extra day, he would be frantic with no way to find out what had happened. In spite of not sleeping the night before, I could not let go of my worry, and my excitement, dashed by fatigue and frustration, had turned to anger. So, I read, fighting to focus, continually having to re-read whole pages.

Meanwhile, John had wangled a 24-hour pass to surprise me in Luxembourg. With no knowledge of the German language and no familiarity with the train system, he had bought an express ticket to Luxembourg. Somehow, in the confusion of platforms and tracks and advice given in German, John ended up on a slow train stopping everywhere, rather than the express. Based on travel he had experienced in Iowa, he never dreamed there would be multiple trains going to the same destination. He began to worry that he would not make it to Luxembourg before I arrived and left on the bus since I had no idea he was coming. Other passengers, usually with a bit of English, helped him transfer trains twice before he made it to Luxembourg.

He grinned and sighed in relief when he saw the posting of my flight delay. He had not missed my arrival. New arrival time "07:00," enough time for dinner. But it didn't dawn on him until after he ate, in Europe 07:00, like army time, meant seven o'clock in the morning, not in the evening. Europeans wrote seven o'clock in the evening as 19:00. The notice definitely said 07:00, not 19:00. He was crushed. I would not arrive until seven o'clock the next morning, and he could not stay. His 24-hour pass would expire overnight, so he had to return to Mannheim without me or be AWOL.

Luckily, when I did arrive in Luxembourg, even with the flight delay, the bus that connected with the Icelandic flight stood ready to depart for Mannheim, a four to five-hour trip. By now I had wrinkles in my dress, runs in my nylons, blisters on my heels, mascara under my eyes, and once again I would greet John with my Mary-Tyler-Moore flip having flopped. No matter!

On the bus I saw little of the countryside. My head bobbled against the window as I succumbed to fatigue, but I had made it to Europe, on my own. As we entered Mannheim, I awoke from my stupor thinking about how I was to find John. There was no such thing as a cell phone or email. I had no work address or telephone number. All I did have was our apartment address: 102 Arndtstrasse, Mannheim-Feudenheim. A slip of paper. The bus would leave me at the Mannheim Hauptbahnhof, the main train station. Once there, I reasoned, I could find a currency exchange inside and get some dollars changed to Deutschmarks for a taxi. At a train station, taxis should be easy to find. With the address in writing, I could show it to the cabbie, no need to speak German. I realized John might not be home, most likely would be on duty. Hopefully, the landlady would be there to let me in. I knew *Frau* was "Mrs" in German. I could say, "Frau Paul," and point to myself. I could show her the address, too. Hopefully, she would understand, in spite of my muddled mind and chaotic appearance. That was my plan. But I refused to think about the possibility of hours sitting on the front curb, with my luggage and without a bed or bath, waiting for John to return.

As it happened, when the bus stopped in front of the Mannheim train station, I saw John out my window looking anxious, but gorgeous to me, in his baggy, grease-smeared fatigues, filthy from motor pool duty. A superior officer had taken pity, and John, again without speaking German, had found my bus and me—somehow. It was another movie moment, rushing into each other's arms, right there in the middle of the day in the middle of downtown Mannheim, no concern for decorum or luggage trailing behind. He took me to our new home and immediately had to return to duty. But I had arrived! I had found John! Sometimes youth means acting impetuously, too stupid to be afraid. At such times, with some luck, wanting something to the core of your being, can vitalize you to produce some kind of miracle. At least that's how I felt.

Dear Folks,

I took the train from Mannheim to Luxembourg to meet Pat, to find her plane had been "delayed" <u>14 hours.</u> . . . On my way back now; sure hope I can find her some day.

Love John

PS I've got her now!

—John W Paul,
postmarked 2 Sep 1969,
APO 09028

Finding Pat

BOOK THREE

◆━━━◆

FEDERAL REPUBLIC OF GERMANY

MAP: Post-World War II Germany

12

◆━━━━◆

Discombobulation

September 1969: A Gallup Poll finds that 55% of Americans think the US made a mistake sending troops to fight in Vietnam.

September 2, 1969: Ho Chi Minh, President of North Vietnam, dies. His family has him embalmed and put on display in a mausoleum in Hanoi.

Our new home was in post-World War II Germany, formerly the German Third Reich under Adolph Hitler, now 24 years later. Following the war, at the Potsdam Conference on July 17, 1945, the victorious Allies divided the German homeland and its capital Berlin into four zones administered by the British, French, Soviets, and the US respectively. The British, French, and Americans soon joined their territories, including their sectors in Berlin, into a new country, the Federal Republic of Germany, a liberal democracy commonly referred to as West Germany with its capital in Bonn. The Soviet's zone and their sector of Berlin became the German Democratic Republic or East Germany and East Berlin with an authoritarian communist government like the Soviets. Thus, for most of the second half of the 20th century, democratic Germany stood next to communist Germany, a country divided.

From 1945–1952 the US Army occupied Germany, initially providing humanitarian aid, later helping set up the new government, and eventually priming the economy with monetary aid through the Marshall Plan. A destitute, dependent Germany and Japan became a drag on the US economy, so their recovery and prosperity benefitted Americans. Thus, my father, tongue-in-cheek, always said: "One of the best things that can happen to a country is losing a war with the US." If taken seriously, that is crass and callous considering the human loss and destruction of war. However, US actions provided a sharp contrast to the Soviet occupying forces who pilfered the industries of East Germany for the reparations they felt they deserved. Although the German economy in the West recovered more quickly than in the East, most Germans disliked the US programs of denazification and the Nuremberg War Trials.

After 1952 the US role evolved into a Cold War presence to protect Germany from the Soviets as part of the North Atlantic Treaty Organization (NATO). We all knew that the forces stationed there and elsewhere in Europe represented a token response. NATO hoped their troops, including those of the US, might slow down an invading army until reinforcements arrived, but mostly we presented a deterrent and a dare, a dare we hoped no one would take. If the communists chose to invade, they would have to kill American soldiers and trigger World War III.

The army even pulled in the wives as we were briefed on identifying spy vehicles from East Germany by their license plates and reporting their whereabouts if spotted. While it was legal for them to be in West Germany, the US wanted to know exactly where they went and what interested them. Being sitting ducks was our role to play, our mission, and it did beat fighting in the jungle! PS: Although I tried to be vigilant, I never saw an East German car.

Like Dorothy, no longer on her aunt's farm in Kansas, I knew we were no longer on John's family farm in Iowa. In Germany workmen wore lederhosen, knicker-length, not bib coveralls. Horses, not tractors, often pulled farm wagons. The billboards were round, and *Strassenbahns*, or streetcars, rattled along the city streets instead of buses, along with the Volkswagen Bugs, some Audis and BMWs, and the occasional Mercedes. When sirens wailed, they sounded like the Gestapo in a World War II movie. Who knew that sirens made a different noise in Europe?

Even trees were different. Yes, they came in deciduous and coniferous like at home, but somehow the branching patterns, the leaves, the needles, and the pine cones were not quite the same. Looking to the sky above, something we expect as a constant in our world, the cloud patterns appeared different, too. A look at landscape paintings from the Old Masters confirms this. Thank goodness, a rose was still a rose, and smelled as sweet, by the same name in German and English. Our landlady, Frau Schaeffer, grew masses of climbing roses along the wall next to the path leading from her front gate to her front door. Often, we had to wrestle prickly branches out of our way. We called it Frau Schaeffer's "Rose Jungle," and we did stop to smell the roses as we approached our apartment.

We entered by the same front door as she did. Let me take you in. Be prepared for an adventure. Open the door and step across the threshold into her entry. You will face four closed doors, closed to preserve the scant heat in each of her main floor rooms: her living room, dining room, study, and kitchen. To get to our apartment, we must climb the first flight of stairs rising from the entry, then traverse a landing and climb another flight that arrives at four more closed doors: Frau Schaeffer's three bedrooms plus her bathroom. Again, we must climb, traverse another landing, and finally mount the last flight of stairs arriving at our own landing facing our four closed doors: our living room, bedroom, kitchen, and bath. Be careful looking down over the rickety railing. It's not for the faint of heart. One push could send the bad guy in a B-grade movie spiraling to certain death splayed on the entry floor, four flights of stairs below.

Once up in our garret under the eaves, all four outside walls slant toward a midpoint above, where they meet in the center of the roof. It's impossible to place the furniture against a wall or to walk within three or four feet of the outside edge of any room unless you are a toddler, yet I must dust, scrub, wax, and polish the floors all the way to the wall.

Our apartment, unlike that of our friends Louise and Nolan, has hot running water. We don't need to boil water to wash dishes. Each sink, both kitchen and bathroom, has its own water heater, small and attached to the wall nearby. And we don't need to build a fire in the bathroom water heater an hour before we want a bath. We only have to remember to turn on our water heater an hour before. Granted, we don't have much hot water. When the entire tank is tempered with a bit of cold, it fills to only a few inches in the bottom of the clawfoot bathtub. But we don't have to carry firewood up all those stairs and build a fire either.

In our living room, we sink into our nubby, once rose-colored sofa till we practically sit on the floor. Frau Schaeffer has wrapped a floral-patterned throw around the seat cushions to keep the loose stuffing from coming out of the worn fabric. The formerly grand Asian carpet has only the weft and woof strings remaining in the thinnest patches with the brown linoleum floor clearly visible beneath. Who knows what the rug design used to be? The original colors in the wrinkled wallpaper have faded to aged yellows and tans with a few water marks, and the top corners of each strip, having lost their adhesion and succumbed to gravity, peel from the wall, now curled and rolled and clogged with dust, dangling from above.

Our German bed, like two twins pushed together, has, instead of two twin mattresses, three sections of mattress per bed. Two of our six total mattress sections are too wide for the bed frame and don't fit. We have placed one of these at the foot of each bed so the bottom third of each twin tilts toward the other. That way the slant, being at our feet, makes the least impact on our ability to sleep, and we both share the discombobulation equally. This arrangement, however, only occurred after experimentation and negotiation. And we have no closet, only *Schränken*, German wardrobes, for our hanging clothes and shoes plus a dresser out on the landing for our undies.

Ah, and I save the kitchen for last. Step in. As you can see, the fridge is the size of a bar fridge at home with no freezer and, therefore, no ice. We still buy meat at the Commissary and keep it for a week even though it becomes brown. Looking back, I can't believe we escaped food poisoning. The stove burners and oven are gas powered and must be lit with a match. The heat control goes from less to more or back to less. We buy an oven thermometer and hang it from the back of the shelf in order to have a rough idea about the temperature. Of course, it registers Celsius, so we learn to convert: 180 degrees Celsius equals 350 degrees Fahrenheit. I mailed our toaster, blender and a hand mixer, wedding presents, to Germany before I came myself, but they operate on 120-volt electricity. Germany uses 240 volts, and the plugs and outlets are a different configuration. We must buy a transformer and plug adapters. And we have no built-in cupboards, only a sideboard for all of our dishes, utensils, pots and pans, appliances, linens, and food pantry— everything.

John lived there. I loved it. But I knew the financial ability to stay there depended on my finding a job.

13

Shifting

September 24, 1969: The Chicago 7 are indicted for violating anti-riot laws in connection with the 1968 Democratic Convention.

"Okay, so you have to put it in first gear to start from a dead stop. Can you do that much?" A grinding noise resulted. "Oh, my god. You're going to BLOW the transmission. To move the shift, you have to have the pedal pushed down all the way. Try it again."

As I fought the tears that I knew would only make the situation worse, I tried to push the pedal through the floor to the cement below.

"Okay, you've got the pedal down. Now move the stick into first. No, no, damn it! That's reverse up there. It's like an H, except reverse, which is up and to the left."

So, it was great to be together again!

Instead of chugging around the pasture in Iowa, now, on Sunday when the PX and Commissary were closed, we lurched around the empty parking lot. I had to master the stick shift in our new car, a spiffy silver Opel Kadet Rallye which John had bought from an officer headed back to the states. I could take the strassenbahn from our apartment into downtown or even to Turley Barracks, home of John's 537th MP Company, but I needed to drive to the PX and Commissary for American goods and groceries with labels and directions in English. Most importantly, I hoped to drive to work, wherever that might be.

On John's first day off, instead of enjoying our new surroundings, he drove me to the Mannheim American High School, the nearest Department of Defense school. I had no idea if my application, transcripts, and fingerprints had ever landed in Mannheim. Although school had already started, in my rosy optimism, I hoped they had a shortage of teachers like at home or more students than expected. Neither proved true. Not only that, but I learned that wives of enlisted personnel would not be considered for regular positions because their spouses could be transferred suddenly. Transferred suddenly?

"To where?" I asked.

"Why, to Nam, of course."

I didn't believe that could apply to us. John's status at the 537th wasn't temporary. Right now, my problem was money, finding a job, so I sought out the civil service hiring office, thinking I could still work as a secretary. Hopefully, they had received my application and test results. My next new learning: the Status of Forces Agreement gave hiring priority to German citizens. It didn't matter if I could type 10 words per minute or 110 words per minutes, army employers couldn't consider me if any minimally qualified German applicant existed. Although World War II had ended almost a generation ago, the German economy was still clawing its way back from total devastation. Indeed, evidence included the occasional piles of rubble left from the war and those farmers who still relied on horse-drawn wagons to bring their produce to the markets in town. Many people needed jobs, especially good-paying jobs, such as those offered by the US government in Germany.

After these depressing developments, I even applied at the Berlitz language school in Mannheim to teach English as a Second Language, but they didn't need anyone either. They asked me what accent I had. I had no idea. I spoke American English, and I wasn't from the South or Boston or Brooklyn. To my ear we midwesterners spoke just plain English. That wasn't the right answer. I didn't realize we "worshed" our clothes or went fishing in the "crick."

So, I wasn't driving to work, but that first month in Germany, I did learn to drive a stick-shift, kind of, so that I could have the car for shopping and errands. John started taking the strassenbahn to work some days, in uniform, of course. The army intended for an MP with his gear to look intimidating, and when he put on a frowny face, he did. He wore a white dress hat with a black-patent brim, encircled in gold braid. Pinned in the center front, a brass US eagle glared down, as if to say, "Mess with me at your peril." A heavy black belt with a shoulder strap hung over his green wool, dress-uniform jacket. From the belt dangled the tools of his trade, handcuffs, a night stick, extra ammo, and a large, but empty holster which would hold the MP's signature .45 caliber pistol issued at the station. His tall black boots held the bottoms of his green dress trousers, tucked in to accentuate the boots, laced, spit-shined, and brutal. He wore a brassard, a black cloth band, around his upper left arm. It displayed his battalion badge, a griffin, the mythological symbol of vigilance and preparedness, as in preparedness for war, and the over-sized white letters: *MP*. A generous amount of insignia, brass buttons, white braid, and expert marksmanship medals completed "the look."

Imagine him stepping onto a streetcar in West Germany in 1969. He would climb the stairs, validate his ticket in the machine next to the driver, and start down the center aisle looking for an empty seat. Immediately, he would realize that all eyes were on him, everyone worrying: "Will the American MP sit next to me?" He would, of course, take an empty seat if available. However, he often had to sit next to someone. They invariably got up and stood or sat with someone else. So, after this happened several times, if the streetcar was crowded, he stood and hung on to the ceiling strap. Still he could feel the eyes. It was always worse when he made the necessary transfer to a second strassenbahn, located nearer the city center and, therefore, always crowded.

Even though US troops no longer acted as an army of occupation, it didn't mean they were popular. And the German *Polizei*, who John patrolled with on occasion, were not popular either as the German people didn't have our many civil liberties and protections. John never used his night stick, but the German officers frequently did, on their fellow Germans. Being an American MP in West Germany would lead to many adventures and lessons learned, chronicled hereafter. One of our earliest lessons became the need for John to avoid public transportation in uniform. He needed to have the car.

As the fall wore on, we started to worry. If we couldn't afford our apartment, I would have to go home to live with my parents, and John would have to move back into the barracks with the single guys. Luckily, the Mannheim American High School eventually retrieved my application materials from the Department of Defense bureaucracy and wanted me to substitute. It wouldn't be regular or dependable. It might be just enough. But we had no telephone for them to notify me. How would they contact me? Graciously, Frau Schaeffer allowed us to receive calls from the school on her phone. Of course, that also helped us to pay her monthly rent.

My routine went like this: I got up at 5:30 am and got ready for school. If the phone rang between 6:00 and 7:00 am, Frau Schaeffer would not answer knowing it was for me. While getting ready, I would listen for the ringing two floors below with our doors open to the unheated hall. Once I heard a ring, I ran down the staircase, slid across the linoleum landings, through her entry hall, rushing to open her study door. I dove for the phone centered on a yellowed lace doily atop her ornately-carved telephone stand. When I got an assignment for the day, I would have to place an outgoing call for a taxi, and then record each call in a pocket-sized spiral we kept on her phone stand. Each call cost 20 *Pfennig*, one-fifth of a Deutschmark, which we reimbursed to Frau Schaeffer.

I subbed for any subject including band and boys' PE. Desperation! If the kids were difficult, I blamed it on the regular teacher and laughed all the way to the bank. Although I worked more days than any other substitute that year, on the many mornings when the phone didn't ring, I consoled myself by returning to bed, like a movie star, with coiffured hair and make-up.

Stick Shift

14

STRAC

October 15, 1969: In Boston Senator George McGovern speaks to the crowd at the National Moratorium Against the War demonstration, the largest protest ever held in the city's history.

I pulled aside the tattered lace curtain to watch out our front window for John returning for lunch after his morning in the motor pool. MPs when they patrolled "PM's," or "swing shifts," from three in the afternoon to eleven o'clock in the evening, had to serve time each morning as grease monkeys keeping their jeeps street-worthy. The army preferred jeeps for MP street patrol because they aligned with the troops' primary mission: to provide the first line of defense in case of a Soviet-backed invasion. Street sedans, although faster and more stable for police duties, would be nearly useless in combat; jeeps, however, had that macho all-terrain capability. So, the MPs on swings spent their mornings washing jeeps, changing their oil and fluids, replacing tires, switching out parts, and making simple repairs.

At last I spotted the Opel turning the corner, then pulling up over the curb to park German style, right wheels on the sidewalk. I hurried to the bathroom to turn on the water heater above the bathtub and then into the kitchen to light with a match both of the gas burners, one under the tomato soup and the other under the toasted-cheese sandwiches. By then I could hear John's boots on the stairs, no sneaking up on anyone in those clunkers.

As he approached the landing and our four closed doors, he called, "Pat? Pat? Where are you?"

"In here, the kitchen," I answered, anticipating the best part of my day. I felt like the prize behind one of the doors on the TV show "Let's Make a Deal."

He crossed to where I stood tending the soup and sandwiches, and from behind he threaded his hands underneath my arms, around my waist, and patted my tummy where we hoped a new family addition might be growing. He pulled my back against him with a squeeze and bent in to kiss my ear from behind.

When the sandwiches turned light brown, I scooped them onto a plate and poured the warm soup into our chipped bowls, setting both on our plastic placemats with our mismatched spoons. Always being cold in the apartment, I sipped the hot liquid loudly and with gusto, but John toyed with a cracker at the bottom of his.

"Bad news today," he sighed, eyes lowered. "The 539th, our sister company, got orders for Nam . . . the whole outfit . . . every last man . . . whether they have 12 months or 12 days left to serve."

My stomach, so hungry seconds earlier, wanted to toss back the soup. "How can they do that? Why would you pay to send a soldier all that way if he were just coming home in a month or less?"

"The army's not about making sense. Remember "SNAFU". . . Situation Normal, All F***ed Up? This makes as much sense as the guys we've known who've gotten orders for Nam out of the blue. Some of them were short-timers, too."

Not knowing whether to scream or cry, I sucked in my breath and released it slowly, "Sooo, the bottom line is we're never safe until you have your discharge in hand?"

Now he raised his eyes to mine, "That's about the size of it. All we can do is enjoy each day and see what happens," he replied, looping a loose lock of my hair behind my ear. So Carpe Diem became our mantra. The silver lining: each day together became more precious, each others' jokes more hilarious, each touch more electric.

I squeezed his hand and kissed him on the cheek. Now I understood why the school wouldn't hire enlisted wives because their husbands could be transferred suddenly. Here came the Elephant again, just when we thought we had banished him. By day he leered at us from the shadows, and at night he lurked under our bed, not romping in the open, but never far away.

I left the lunch mess for later and went to check the water heater in the bathroom. Finding it hot, I called across the landing, "You get undressed. I'll take care of filling the tub." That might be a simple job at home but required close attention here. The water heater had to be turned off at just the right moment. Letting the water run too long, allowed the water heater to empty and then run cold water in with the hot. Considering the cold day and cold in the apartment, hot water was imperative. As soon as I felt the water begin to cool, I turned it off. The tub held all of three inches of water.

"John, it's ready," I yelled loud enough for him to hear through the closed bedroom door. Courtesy of the motor pool, he had grease in the lines of his hands, under his nails, somehow on his face, and even in his hair. Once he was in the water, I took the plastic pitcher, filled it from the tub, and poured it over his head. He worked in the shampoo which helped to clean his hands and nails as well. I dumped another pitcher full over his head for the rinse.

Gurgling, he yelped, "I think you're enjoying this a bit too much, my love."

In no time the water turned dark, so more scrubbing became pointless.

While he dried off, I was quickly setting up the ironing board to press his dress shirt and to sharpen the crease in his Class A pants. Clad in his undies, he set to spit-shining his boots rubbing on shoe polish with rags ripped from his army-issue long underwear. Back in basic training, he hadn't thought he would need thermal long-johns in Nam. As he buffed the toe, he spit on it which coaxed a mirror-like shine to slowly, emphasis on slowly, emerge from the leather. Then came the Brasso, with its toxic fumes, applied with more scraps of long underwear, to his belt-buckle, brass lapel pins and the brass eagle on his hat until they all shone, too. Military policemen in Europe had greater responsibility than their counterparts in the US due to the Status of Forces Agreement. The US was committed to support all law enforcement activities relating to US troops stationed in Germany. For the patrol officer this included criminal investigations, patrol of off-

112

post areas, vehicle registration, and traffic-accident investigation among other matters. MP's had to look "STRAC," army slang for a sharp appearance, because they apprehended officers as well as enlisted men, so it was important to project authority.

And now the good-bye kiss as he was on his way although I felt like he had only just arrived. Again, I watched from our window tucked in the eves as he waved and the Opel pulled away. Then I retreated to the kitchen to clean up before deciding how to fill the empty hours until he would return at eleven-thirty that night.

Although asleep, I became aware in the dark that John was stealthily creeping under the feather tick into his side of the bed.

"What time is it?" I sputtered grabbing the alarm clock from the night stand.

He always teased me about how closely I watched that clock when he returned after swing shifts. He spent those evenings in a world wholly foreign to his Iowa farm-boy upbringing. His partner was Duke, a black Detroit street kid, cocky, savvy, and bristling with attitude: John's polar opposite. Their patrol duty included Lupinenstrasse, ironically named after one of my favorite alpine flowers, the lupine, that spreads blue across a high meadow as if reflecting the sky above. The entrance to Lupinenstrasse, closed off and hidden behind overlapping brick walls, protected the innocent, for Lupinenstrasse held the red-light district of Mannheim where prostitution was legal. Being a forbidden, yet favorite, off-duty location for many

GIs meant frequent calls for the MPs. Alcohol often played a role, stoking belligerent behavior, but more often than fights, soldiers simply passed out after their exertion and needed to be removed from the premises. Brothels weren't hotels. For the ladies' time equaled money.

The MPs, STRAC in their pressed uniforms and spit-shined boots, were popular with the "ladies" of the street who considered them their bouncers and liked to express their gratitude for that protection by offering beer or cognac or affection. Duke being Duke, he had not one, but three girlfriends on the strasse, so his patrols never ended without checking on all of them and making plans to return. He strutted down the street charming each girl displayed in her picture window by cooing, "Ish leeba dish," the GI bastardization of "I love you" in German. On the MPs hips, their impressive Colt .45s, cannons compared to the German Polizei's sleek Walthers, also attracted attention from curious German customers. When the inevitable crowd gathered watching Duke in action, he would sense John's nervousness and say under his breath, "Don't worry, college boy, I got your back." And he always did.

Through my fog of interrupted sleep, I saw that the alarm clock said 11:30 on the dot.

"Hi, honey. It's me. I'm home," John whispered as he recovered my open book from under the comforter and brushed my forehead with a kiss. "You must have fallen asleep reading."

Realizing he was home *exactly* on time, I mumbled, "Oh, sweet patootle . . . love you."

15

◆—————◆

Heidelberg Dueling

October 24, 1969: Willy Brandt is elected Chancellor of West Germany and revalues the Deutschmark against the US Dollar. Historically, the dollar has been worth four marks, but now it buys only 3.6 marks, a 10 percent loss in purchasing power for Americans buying goods or services with Deutschmarks.

"John, sweet patootle, it's nearly 11:00." I had prefaced these remarks with a few delicate kisses traced across his sleeping brow. "We need to get a move on if we're going to Heidelberg," I prompted.

"What? What? Move, where? Just let me sleep!" He pulled his pillow over his head.

Lifting the corner of the pillow, I whispered, "We need to get moving, actually you need to get moving, before another day slips away from us."

He had spent the previous day sleeping. I couldn't blame him. He worked three-day shifts, three swing shifts with motor pool duty in the mornings, and three night shifts, nine days straight. Then he had three days off to enjoy. Joke! After that schedule his body clock had no idea what time of day it was, so all he wanted to do was sleep. For myself, I mostly spent my time alone in the apartment. I had just spent three days creeping around so as not to disturb my sleeping husband who had worked the night shift. Then a fourth day while he slept recovering

115

from rotation. I was ready to roll, to explore, to discover. Having been to Europe before, I had some idea of what we were missing.

Although we lived in Feudenheim, it was a suburb of Mannheim, a city of 330,000 at the confluence of the Neckar River and the Rhine, Europe's second largest inland port, shipping and receiving goods from elsewhere in Germany as well as England, Holland, Switzerland, France, and the Scandinavian countries. The picturesque barges plied the rivers, many still family-operated, the laundry flapping from a line onboard. Having grown up two blocks from the Mississippi River, I found this a comforting, familiar sight, except for the laundry. Downtown Mannheim held a bustling shopping district with both C&A and Kaufhof department stores as well as a central market bursting with picture-perfect produce and cacophony of colorful *Blumchen*, flowers. Mannheim's tourist attractions were limited to the *Residenz*, a 1700's palace of the Electors Palatinate, and to the gardens and ornamental fountains surrounding the Mannheim *Wasserturm* or Water Tower, the city's landmark. And just beyond, in opposite directions, Heidelberg Castle and the Cathedral at Worms beckoned.

My boredom and frustration from being cooped up in our apartment ran deep. I needed to get out there, but so did he! Nothing but working and sleeping would take its toll on his morale, too. Castles, cathedrals, and vineyards awaited! So, I persisted, and he awakened.

The drive to Heidelberg, the logical first attraction for someone with a Heidelberg dueling scar, was 20 kilometers or *klicks* in GI slang, that's only about 12 miles. Yet it took almost an hour as we negotiated the tangle of German roads without many street signs. We couldn't tell what road or street we were on which made following our map futile. Once in the Heidelberg city limits, after several wrong turns, we still didn't know how to find the castle and old town. We had no idea. We didn't know the German word for castle, *Schloss,* or for old town, *alte Stadt,* or downtown, *Stadtmitte.* John, of course, true to form, showed stellar patience with my navigational skills. We tried following the Neckar River which eventually wound its way to the arched spans of the Old Bridge, leading into the old town. And 300 feet above, there it stood on a hillside overlooking the river, Heidelberg Castle, a vivid contrast to its deep green surroundings with its red sandstone aglow in the afternoon sun. Clumps of brilliant red fall leaves just beginning to turn created border patterns as if to frame the image. Thus, began our love affair with Heidelberg Castle, and indeed, with all of the feudal castles we have visited since.

We strolled across the cobble-stoned bridge, constructed of the same red sandstone as the castle, stopping for a photo in front of the monumental sculpture of Minerva in flowing neoclassical robes built on a balcony extending out over one side of the river. The goddess of wisdom seemed appropriate; Heidelberg was a university town. At the end of the bridge, we walked through an arch, barely large enough for a VW Bug, topped with twin, onion-domed towers. Framed by the arch, ancient stone and stucco buildings, most with terra cotta tiled roofs, covered the hillside beyond, sprinkled with spires and domes. Entering old Heidelberg felt like we had walked into our own fairytale. Could we be awake? Who would have thought when John joked about his Heidelberg dueling scar that we would soon live near Heidelberg? We picked up signs with a castle icon pointing up the hill. This romantic, cobble-stoned path climbed through vaulted passages and old tunnels, beneath palaces and mansions, until we emerged high above the city into the manicured castle yard. Magnificent buildings surrounded and overwhelmed us. A conglomeration of styles stood one against the other, reflecting the period and taste of the prince or elector, as the Germans called him, who built each. But the most stunning buildings represented an interpretation of Renaissance architecture in Germany during the 16th and 17th centuries.

"Look at that!" John called out pointing to the Ottheinrich Building. "The guy who built that knew how to live. . . But looks like it didn't last forever!"

The facade reflected the antique Roman building style with the first floor being most monumental and each story above becoming lighter, less grand in scale, but retaining much of the ornamentation. Twisted columns framed some windows while fluted columns framed others. Vines of fruit wound above and between the windows. Pedestals and niches held stone sculptures which would have been a job to count. And above the raised entrance a sculptured heraldic panel including Otto Heinrich himself told all who entered beneath that they entered his house. But the most striking feature of the facade was the blue sky framed by the empty windows of the two roofless upper stories. It was a surrealistic effect, a view of heaven beyond, that no amount of carved stone could convey.

"How do you 'spose that happened," I asked?

John philosophized, "Some days it might have been good to be the elector, but maybe not every day."

"But what about all the folks who never got to be the elector, or the king, but had a bad day following his orders?"

"I'm guessing lots of his soldiers had some really bad days fighting his wars, lined up facing bowmen or in hand-to-hand combat with broadswords and axes," John noted.

A promenade of the outer walls led to what became one of our favorite sights: the Powder Tower. The outer wall, blown away, rested below, intact, in the now-dry moat, in one huge, solid chunk, as if it were merely a broken pottery shard. It left a gaping opening that revealed three stories of powder chambers. Today ivy wound around the structure as if some giant was trying to tie the pieces back together, and the late afternoon sun turned the autumnal red foliage into another kind of blaze.

"The day that exploded prob'ly wasn't a great day for the elector or his troops either," I proclaimed. On the other hand, it would have been a great day for a princess when the Elizabeth Gate, a charming ornamental stone arch in the gardens, was built overnight as a surprise present on the occasion of the Electoress Elizabeth's 19th birthday.

With glee we made our last stop on our first castle tour: a visit to the *Weinstube* or great vat, built in the cellar, with a dance floor mounted on top. Actually, three barrels formerly existed to hold the wine tithe paid by farmers to their reigning Houses. Pumps brought the "liquid of kings" to the Royal Hall or the Terrace.

John gasped, "Imagine the party you could throw with that. Makes a kegger look pretty puny." I could tell he was not miles but years away, imagining himself living the life of an elector, wine glass in hand.

So, on his next three-day hiatus, we took a jaunt to Worms, around 35 klicks or 20 miles up the Rhine. John knew the way because his MP company had a detachment there, and he had had to fill in occasionally. We headed for the famous Worms Cathedral where the Diet of Worms in 1521 declared Martin Luther a heretic, thus jump-starting the Protestant Reformation in Germany. American world history students, if they remember nothing else, remember the "Diet of Worms." Ooo, gross and disgusting! The Diet was an assembly of the Holy Roman Empire held at St. Peter's Cathedral in the town of Worms, Germany. None of those fat fathers, who according to Martin Luther grew rich from selling pardons for their sins to poor people, ate worms. But they undoubtedly drank a good deal of great German wine!

The Romanesque cathedral, at once both humbling and awe-inspiring, worked its magic on us as its architects had intended. Made of the same elegant red sandstone as Heidelberg Castle, its length extended far enough to enclose a football field. Five towers enticed us to look heavenward. Stained-glass windows created patterns in the stone surrounded with statues and gargoyles to keep the devil away. Portions of the exterior existed from the original edifice begun in 1110, way before Columbus, and only 100 years after the Viking explorer Leif Eriksson, perhaps, discovered America. Additions to the building continued into the 14th century, and repairs of war damage from the Reformation and French Revolution were made in the 17th and 18th centuries. Taken all together they reflected the changes in artistic styles and periods from the Romanesque through the Baroque. A thorough renovation of the interior and exterior took place from the time of our Civil War into the Depression years only to have the roof damaged again from World War II Allied bombing—that's us—in the spring of 1945, only 10 years later. The place was a three-dimensional timeline of Western Civilization and art history.

The enormity of the interior dwarfed us, making our human concerns petty and inconsequential compared to the affairs of God. The massive granite columns lifted our eyes to the vaulted ceiling taller than the tree tops outside. Angled rays of sunshine from the arched windows just below the ceiling flooded in as if sent straight from God in person. The stone itself exuded strength and provided a staid backdrop against which the ornately carved, wooden, Baroque-style choir and high altar danced in their golden splendor dazzling us.

What if we had been peasants passing through that portal? No wonder they tithed to the church from the pittance they made. No wonder they bought indulgences to gain God's forgiveness. Who could have argued with the majesty of God emanating from his Cathedral? Only Martin Luther, who risked his life to stop the abuses of the church. Once again, I caught that faraway look in John's eye as he mentally traveled in time, imagining the pompous proceedings of the church bishops, rotund and bald-headed, garbed in robes of white and red and gold, versus the fearful bravery of a young scholar dressed in humble black, a young man who couldn't deny his conscience.

We were hooked: cathedrals and castles. We have no idea how many we've seen in a lifetime, but they still pull us in as we make our annual pilgrimage to Europe or Asia or South America. When we lived in Scotland, we joked that we needed a bumper sticker: We Brake for Castles. Perhaps they define the moment we began enjoying our life together, not just avoiding Vietnam together.

✛

Heidelberg and Worms

16

Home Alone

November 12, 1969: The news story breaks that the US Army has been covering up the massacre by US soldiers of Vietnamese civilians in My Lai since March of 1968.

November 15, 1969: Largest antiwar protest in American history takes place in Washington, DC, with 250,000- 600,000 (sources vary) peaceful demonstrators.

November 16, 1969: President Nixon promises to withdraw 35,000 additional troops from Vietnam.

November 20, 1969: Members of Indians of All Tribes seize Alcatraz Island demanding a deed to the island and a Native American university and cultural center.

The snow against my window demanded my attention. Was it snowing or was it sleeting? Whatever, it pinged as it hit, but turned quickly into rivulets merging as they wound their way down the pane, blurring the whiteness that lay beyond. For the first time this season the white clung to the empty tree branches and spread over the still-grassy backyards visible from my lofty perch at our kitchen window. The stucco houses ringing the block were quickly losing their separate identities, no longer the protective barrier that separated the giggly, squealing children who played in their backyards from the passersby and cars on the sidewalk and street in front. Now the white roofs joined the white grass to the white streets and sidewalks beyond. Nothing stirred, and quiet prevailed.

Yes, it was peaceful and had its beauty, but the cold seeped in around the peeling, wood-framed window edges and through the thin glass where I could use my fingernail to etch pictures in the icy condensation. Germans had no such thing as storm windows. I could pull down the rolling shutter as I had done in our other rooms, but then I would be entirely closed off from the world around me. I touched the radiator below the window hoping for some warmth, but as usual the metal was as cold as the window and made me involuntarily shiver.

As we became more familiar with German living, we realized that Germans, due to the high cost of natural gas, kept their houses far below the 72 degrees Fahrenheit that we were used to at home. But we didn't know that yet. I kept asking about the heat, not understanding.

"Frau Schaeffer, Frau Schaeffer are you there?" I called over the railing as I clomped down the cracked, linoleum-covered stairs from our apartment, winding past her closed bedroom doors on the landing and then to the first floor below. I knew she must be there as the scent of slightly burning onions and cabbage greeted me in spite of her closed kitchen door. Indeed, she emerged from the kitchen.

"*Guten Tag*, Frau Paul," she said with the Paul sounding more like "Pow-ool" in her German accent. Although it was nearly lunch time, I caught a potent whiff of alcohol on her breath, and she still wore her threadbare chenille robe shuffling across the brown linoleum in her dingy slippers. She immediately began her usual diatribe that accompanied every greeting.

"You know, during the var, I vas just a mother alone with my four children. Vat could I do?" This in spite of the fact that the focal point of her living room was the larger-than-life portrait above the fireplace, her husband in uniform, a colonel in the Luftwaffe.

I never knew how to deal with her guilt. The German aggression and Holocaust were horrifying. But in the war, she had lost her husband and her youngest son who died at home from appendicitis. All of the doctors were at the front. How much responsibility could I place on her personally? I struggled with the individual German's accountability for Hitler and the Holocaust versus the struggles of the people I had met who had suffered severe hardships. Who had been active Nazis? How much did they know? Did anyone resist or were they all complicit? It's hard to hate a whole country of people when you know individuals, and they have paid a high price. How much blame could I put on this old woman? I didn't know what to think as I faced her.

"Frau Schaeffer, there is no heat again from our radiator." I pulled up the hem of my jeans displaying my layers, "See! I have on 2 pairs of sox and a pair of pants under my jeans." I extended my hands, fingers curled back toward my palm, displaying my nails. "My fingernails are blue. If I put on gloves, I can't write or even turn pages to read. What will I do?"

"I called the man," she said shrugging her shoulders and rolling her filmy blue eyes upward. "What more can I do?" She turned back toward the pungent concoction she had cooking on the stove. Months later when I figured out that "the man" didn't exist, I could have held it against Frau Schaeffer for lying to me, but she was a proud, if defeated, woman, and I preferred to think she couldn't admit to the privation that life in post-war Germany demanded for survival.

This day, not wanting to create an international incident, I turned to climb back to my nest in the attic knowing I would have to resort to the gloves. Could I add a second sweater over the turtleneck? Would it fit under John's baggy sweatshirt that I wore over everything? It not only provided warmth, hanging almost to my knees, but his scent gave me comfort when he wasn't there. He was gone to the "field" for the week on maneuvers, Operation REFORAGER the Army called it, living in a pup tent and playing war games, not in the snow, I hoped.

Awkward in my gloves, I turned off the Armed Forces Network radio station that was droning on, the same old news over and over. There was no television to watch. It would have been in German, if we had one, and what was the use of that? It might have brightened my day to talk to my friend Louise, but neither of us had a telephone, so any plans had to be made through our husbands at work. I could never commit ahead of time for fear I would miss a day of subbing, so we seldom were able to get together without our husbands. I had subbed last week, but nothing this week. This morning I had filled the time writing my weekly letter home, 12 pages by hand, no typewriter. I made a carbon copy, as usual, and sent it to John's parents. Next week I would send them the top copy and mail my parents the carbon. Our weekly copy of *Time* magazine had been read from cover to cover days ago, soooo, what to do? I never thought I could possibly have more time than books to read, but when you spend most of your days reading, you can even need a break from that. And now in my gloves, I couldn't turn pages.

Since I couldn't possibly be any colder, I decided to walk to the stores on Feudenheim's Hauptstrasse or main street. It would be something to do. I checked my purse for Deutschmarks and found four, a bit more than a dollar to spend. Exchanging John's sweatshirt for my only coat, I clomped back down the stairs and stepped out the heavy front door. Immediately, I pulled my collar up around my ears and bent my head down in a futile attempt to keep the icy snow, almost hail, from stinging my cheeks. All I could see was the solitary impression I made with each step, adding one to another, making my own trail. Across the street and down the block I crunched, barely able to make out the tan and grey houses as I passed. At the main street, the strassenbahn clanked by on its rails, bell ringing. The lights inside seemed warm and inviting, if only I had some place to go!

I trudged on toward the shops glad to get inside at the *Lebensmittelgeschäft*, the grocers.

"*Guten Morgen*," I greeted the clerk who automatically answered the same without looking up. Due to the weather, the few vegetables that usually sat in boxes outside the door had been stacked inside making entry difficult. The open-air market in downtown Mannheim had beautiful produce, fruits, and flowers, but this was a sorry display starring the ubiquitous German cabbage.

As I moved past the produce and approached the shelves, I looked for familiar items. I couldn't read the German labels, but I knew a can with green beans pictured on the front had to be green beans. I was drawn to the boxes picturing gorgeous iced layer cakes. However, a look on the back at the directions in German, gobbledy-gook to me, discouraged that purchase. With six weeks of travelers' German provided by the US Army for GIs and their dependents, I could say *bitte* and *danke,* recite the days of the week and months of the year, and count to 100. My highest achievement was being able to ask "Where is the train station?" Of course, I couldn't understand anyone's reply with directions to the train station. Eventually, I returned to the lowly cabbage. From my mother-in-law on the farm, I knew how to make escalloped cabbage with Saltines, milk and butter, which came in handy living in Germany. It was cheap, only 50 pfennig.

Next door at the M*etzgerei,* the butcher shop, in spite of the cold, I had to summon my courage to enter as I could barely face the headless and still-feathered chickens hanging in the window along with the single, not too plump, goose. The butcher was thankfully in the back. Ahead the sides of beef, pork, and mutton hung behind the meat case which was filled with sausages: skinny sausages, curved sausages, speckled sausages, lumpy sausages, smooth sausages, pink sausages, on and on. Who knew what was in them, brains, tongue, intestines? But I spied some of the W*eisswurst,* white veal sausages, that were often grilling at open-air markets and fests.

"*Wieviel kosten das? kosten zw*ei?" I stammered awkwardly pointing at the veal wurst as the butcher in his bloody white apron emerged from the rear.

"*Zwei Mark, fünfig,*" he replied slurring the last syllable until it sounded like "ish" in his soft and sloppy southern German dialect. With the price less than a dollar, I bought the two wurst.

Now came the *Bäckerei* or bakery. This was the warmest store of all and the smell of the many baked breads and sweet rolls provided all the temptation that had been lacking at the metzgerei. Since I had cabbage and wursts, I needed a couple of *Brötchen*, the Volkswagen of German breads, crunchy hard rolls, much like miniature rounds of French bread, that Germans serve with their wurst. I had enough change left for two.

And then I headed home, eyes and head down, back hunched against the weather. The hardest part came when I passed the *Konditorei*, the pastry and confection shop, where I peered through the glass at the customers with money lingering on red velvet chairs at small white marble tables drinking their warm cocoas and coffees with gooey slices of black forest cake smothered with *Sahne*, whipping cream. My money spent on the essentials, I trudged with my purchases around the corner, back up the side street, and across to my front door retracing my earlier tracks.

Inside, as it was growing dark anyway, I pulled down the kitchen shutter hoping to insulate myself a bit from the cold. Inside my nest I put yet another can of tomato soup on the stove to warm while I grilled another toasted-cheese sandwich. Affordable comfort food. Soon it would be Thanksgiving, and we would be hosting the holiday for friends and roasting a turkey in our tiny oven. And John had some comp time coming, so we hoped to go to Switzerland for a getaway.

But tonight, I would spend alone under our down comforter, reading. Tomorrow night John and I would have wursts, cabbage, and brotchen for dinner to celebrate his return. Little did I know that it would take four fills of our tub before the water stopped turning black so he would be clean enough to come to the table!

Home from Field Duty

17

Thankful

November 14–24, 1969: Apollo 12 *conducts a successful mission including the second manned landing on the moon.*

When the doorbell rang, I called across the landing to John, "Louise and Nolan are here." Better let him negotiate the flights of stairs to open the front door. I was already into the whiskey sours that John had concocted from the cheap booze purchased at the PX. Germany was a land of beer and white wine, cheaper than the Coca-Cola we could not afford, but Thanksgiving required a splurge. And John had always called me a cheap date: one drink was all I could handle.

After the hugs and "Happy Thanksgivings," I asked Louise, "Have you ever fixed a turkey?"

"Heck, no! Have you?" she exclaimed over her shoulder as she headed for the whiskey sours.

"No, not really, but my cookbook from home was in the box that finally came last week."

My spotless, new *Betty Crocker's New Picture Cookbook,* a wedding present, had a roast turkey on the cover against a sixties' turquoise background. Today the turkey is still there but covered with random splatters and a circular burn from the bottom of a hot pan. The binding cracked and fell off years ago. The pictures, of course, make the grandchildren laugh. But its arrival in Germany by Thanksgiving 1969 was a godsend. Once Louise had her drink, we anxiously scanned the poultry pages in our inebriated state, trying to make sense of stuffing and trussing and basting, but it all swam together in our whiskey-induced fog. Soon our combined fine motor coordination equaled that of a two-year old.

I flipped the page to actual recipes, and there, thankfully, was our solution: "Roasting Turkey in Aluminum Foil. This method shortens roasting time; also prevents spattering of the oven." We skipped right past the first direction: "Prepare turkey for roasting (details on p. 317)" which would have sent us back to the previous page for stuffing and trussing. Instead we went straight for "Place bird on aluminum foil." Here we could enlist help from husbands. And then we jubilantly completed our preparations ourselves with "wrap snugly." We did not spare the aluminum foil. Never was a bird wrapped more snugly.

Now the problem was getting the oven to 450 degrees. First you had to stand on your head to light the pilot light, another good job for husbands. Then you simply turned the one and only knob clockwise away from the notch marked Off. The more heat required, the farther you turned the knob clockwise. Then you waited 15 to 20 minutes, opened the oven door, and stood on your head again to see the temperature indicated on the oven thermometer in the back corner hanging from the only shelf. If it wasn't warm enough, you closed the door, turned the knob some more, and checked back later. And so on.

In another whiskey sour, the oven registered 232 Celsius, the equivalent of 450 Fahrenheit. I opened the door so that John could slide the bird and roasting pan onto the shelf, but the top of the bird smashed into the top of the oven almost sliding the bird onto the floor. Too big! So, this called for a bit of bird-bashing, nothing major, only a few cracked ribs, but at last the bird slid in, and now we had only to wait three hours for it to roast.

Hopefully, Louise and I would sober up enough to fix the trimmings because Nolan and John had invited two other MPs to join us. At that time Louise and I represented the sum total of enlisted wives of the 537th MP company living in-country. The rest of the enlisted MPs would be spending Thanksgiving in the barracks.

When the guys arrived, Rob Miller and Carl Roper, both were delighted to find out we had turkey, but Carl still complained about missing the football games that usually accompanied Thanksgiving festivities for his family. The fellas were quick to devise their own intricate football game using small matchboxes flicked across the kitchen table. This silly substitute for televised football soon developed into regional rivalries intensified by whiskey and beer.

Nolan lit up with a bright idea: "We should be in that new Super Bowl, the Mannheim MPs. Not those wussy Iowa Hawks of yours."

"Super Bowl? That's not college ball, that's the pros, like Vikings versus Chiefs! I wonder if that will become a popular national event, like the Rose Bowl is for college fans. How many whiskey soursth did you have, anywaysth?" John countered deliberately slurring his words. "The way the Vikings and Chiefs are playing, this year's Super Bowl may be the Corn Belt Bowl, Minneapolis versus Kansas City. And I won't be there!!!!!!" Somehow, Louise and I prepared the feast and transformed their football field back into a dining table. I don't remember where we got the two extra chairs, but four soldiers and two wives squeezed around that table barely large enough for two.

Miller, from New Jersey, lifted his glass of German Riesling and offered the first toast: "Here's to the best cooks east of New Jersey."

Nolan, from Massachusetts, was quick to amend that with, "Here's to the most gorgeous cooks east of Massachusetts."

"Here's to the family back in Iowa," John offered, always nostalgic.

Roper raised his glass, "Here's to the country that invented Thanksgiving!"

"Here's to our new family right here in Mannheim," I proclaimed.

Louise chimed in, "And here's to the whiskey sours!"

We washed down, with liberal amounts of Riesling, the best darn turkey I've ever fixed. And then lingered over the pumpkin pie. The hour grew late, and by the time our guests were ready to depart, all of us were filled with *Gemütlichkeit*, the German spirit found at the beer and wine fests.

"Shhhh!" I admonished them as they emerged onto the landing to begin the tromp down the stairs that would take them right past Frau Schaeffer's bedroom door.

Having imbibed too much to take my warning seriously, Louise continued with her good-byes. "Wasn't that the best turkey? Best turkey I ever fixed," she gushed.

"Keep down the noise. Do you want to get us kicked out?" John pleaded gesticulating wildly.

Then Louise dropped her purse onto the first step. In horror we listened as it hit with a "ka-thud" and then rolled to the second step with another "ka-thud" before rolling to the next and the next and the next, faster and faster. Nolan chased after it but lost his footing on the worn-slick linoleum creating an even louder series of "ka-thuds" bouncing to the landing below. Of course, he came to rest, holding the purse high in victory, like he'd just scored a touchdown, right in front of Frau Schaeffer's bedroom door. Five of us totally lost it laughing, not just out loud, but uproariously.

"Shut up, you idiots. We're gonna' get kicked out," John yelled making more noise than any of us.

However much we laughed in our inebriation, we were distraught the next morning. Would Frau Schaeffer boot us out after our raucous Thanksgiving? We could barely afford our apartment, and when the exchange rate had changed, our rent went up by $11.11 a month, enough to stretch us to the limit. Also, we had suffered some costly repairs on the Opel. By then, we had started to think we might be stuck with a lemon. Besides transmission issues, the heater turned on the windshield wipers, and the windshield wipers turned on the headlights. The bottom line: we could have qualified for welfare at home, but that was distributed by the state government. We lived in Germany, not in Iowa or any other state. My substitute pay helped some, but we still feared I would have to go home to live with my parents, and John would have to join Miller, Roper and the others in the barracks.

I dreaded running into Frau Schaeffer on the stairs and tried to avoid her. Each day that passed without her visiting us seemed to indicate that she did not intend to kick us out. Finally, the inevitable happened. As I stepped off the bottom stair on my way to the front door, she emerged from her kitchen.

"Frau Schaeffer, we are so sorry we were noisy Thursday night," I blurted in apology. It was a special holiday, so we had friends in to celebrate together . . . so they would not be alone in the barracks. It was our Thanksgiving, an important family holiday."

"Ja, ja. I know. It vas your Tanksgiving. My daughter, you know, her husband is American GI. Maybe you see big American car parked sometimes?" she pointed to the street out front.

"Frau Schaeffer, we will not be noisy like that again, especially not late at night," I promised.

With a prim smile and twinkling eyes, she replied, "Ven you are young, sometimes to have fun, is necessary to make little noise. You need to meet my son Peter, he your age, ven he comes home for Christmas." I wanted to hug her.

Pat Wins at Matchbox Football

18

—◆—

Peter

*December 1, 1969: The Selective Service System of the US
conducts its first ever lottery for men born from 1944 to
1950 to determine the order of call to military service in
the Vietnam Conflict so that most young men will know
if they are to be drafted or not.*

*December 3–6, 1969: Lieutenant William Calley appears
on the cover of both* Time *and* Newsweek *magazines. He
has been charged as the officer responsible at the My Lai
Massacre.*

John and I stood on the landing of our garret. He
checked his watch while I straightened my hair yet
again. Then we squeezed hands. We awaited the
appearance of Frau Schaeffer and her son Peter, who was
home for the holidays from veterinary school in Munich.
We so longed to meet someone our age. The Germans we
knew, a generation older, spoke little English, and every
man anxiously explained that he had fought on the
Eastern front against the Russians. If we believed all of
them, our American troops would have been able to
march unopposed across the border into Germany, no D-
Day or Battle of the Bulge. So, Peter, fluent in English
according to his mother, was our chance to connect, to
broaden our perspective. We had lots of questions about
Germany, Germans, their culture, what it was like

growing up in post-World War II Germany, and what he thought of the Vietnam Conflict?

Now we could hear footsteps on the stairs.

"*Guten Abend,*" we sang out in greeting flashing our big American smiles.

They both replied in English, "Good evening," nodding politely, but restrained and more formal.

I couldn't believe it was the same Frau Schaeffer, the one who, when dressed, wore black, baggy pants, several sizes too big, and a charcoal wool sweater, polka-dotted with moth holes. Tonight, she wore a gray silk dress, rumpled and faded, but with a lace collar, a dress that had clearly been distinguished many years ago. She obviously had rouged her cheeks, and she wore dress pumps with seamed stockings, unfortunately sagging a bit around her ankles. Peter, on the other hand, with tousled blond hair, over six feet tall, wore traditional lederhosen buckled below the knee and wooden sandals. How classic!

While John ushered them through our living room door, I grabbed the tray with the glasses of German Riesling and my plate of Christmas cookies from the kitchen. Probably Germans would have preferred cheese and fruit after dinner, but my midwestern culture dictated sharing home-baked cookies.

I arrived as John invited them to take a seat. We did know that Germans don't take a seat in your home until formally asked to do so. Peter had to duck and fold himself under the sloping ceiling of our eaves into the couch. Both mother and son sank in nearly to the floor with matching startled expressions.

At this point I wondered if Frau Schaeffer would begin her usual defensive diatribe, born of guilt I supposed. Sure enough. Here it came: "You know, during the var, I vas only a mother, a voman alone with four children, vat could I do?" she shrugged rolling her eyes skyward as if looking for answers.

Peter jumped off the sofa, narrowly missing the ceiling, and stood in front of her yelling down at her. The color rose in his face, bright red, as his distorted mouth spat his words into her face, in German. He probably thought we didn't understand, and we didn't understand much. But I picked out *Schaf* and *Himmel*, sheep and heaven. I had a sense that he was calling her a sheep. As a farm boy, John had explained to his city wife that sheep were easy to move. You only had to get one going the right direction and the others would fall in behind. And I guessed Peter threw in some "What-in-heaven's-name?" phrases with it. Although most of it was lost in translation, the anger was not.

We were stunned. We had never even imagined talking to our parents like that, let alone in front of other people. We might not agree with them from time to time, especially during the teen years, but we always had respect. This young generation of Germans had to grow up as toddlers thinking their parents knew everything and were always right, only to find out, as they came of age, about the Holocaust, never mind the German aggression of World War II, including the shame and bitterness of defeat. Whether their parents were actively involved in the Nazi machine or merely complicit like sheep, what a burden! What must it be like to grow up in a world without respecting your parents, without regarding your parents as a moral compass and anchor? What depth of emotion separated this mother and son, probably separated many German parents and children!

Peter, finished with his tirade, stormed off, stomping back down the stairs, and she, after struggling to extricate herself from the depths of the sofa, apologized to us over and over, meekly trailing behind him. John, with a look of horror on his face, reminded me that Frau Schaeffer had just the day before invited us to Christmas Eve dinner with her family. Would Peter be there?

✦

My country, right or wrong;
if right, to be kept right;
and if wrong, to be set right.

—Senator Carl Schurz,
The Congressional Globe 1872

Nazi Party Rally 1934

Certainly any one who has the power to
make you believe absurdities has the
power to make you commit injustices.

—Voltaire, *Questions
sur les Miracles* 1765

142

19

Over the Alps

"I think it goes that way, through those trees," I said to
John. He turned the wheel and the car fish-tailed at
first but gradually gripped the snow and crunched in the
direction I was pointing. He had four days straight of
comp time from working extra shifts so we were trying out
our "new" car, a scum-grey, 17-year-old VW Bug, on a
getaway to Switzerland.

"Geez," he said, "I can't see anything but snow!"

"No, kidding," I said trying to peer through the giant
flakes.

We rounded a curve next to what could have been a
picturesque babbling mountain stream by day, but by
night the helter-skelter stacks of ice made the cold feel
even colder. Our headlights struck a large road sign
propped along what we thought was the side of the road.

"Can you make that out?" he asked.

"Only a few letters," I replied being the German
language expert with my six weeks of classes.

"Looks like maybe an *o* and an *s*, maybe two *s*'s," I
guessed. Most of the sign reflected sparkling white in the
headlights from the wet, blowing snow plastered to it. I
thought *Schneekristall*. I did know the German word for
these sparkling snow crystals, but those weren't double *e*'s
on that sign.

"Any clue what it says?" John asked.

"None. Absolutely none!"

"Do you have your dictionary?"

"Are you kidding? How could I see it in the dark and what would I look up anyway with only a few letters from the middle of a word?"

We mushed on in the dark. The road always climbed and never ran straight. Sometimes the headlights reflected off shimmering, snow-covered trees or rocks on one side of the road or the other, but often we could only sense the pure darkness of infinite empty space just beyond the side of the road. Our silence filled the car.

After a long while, John broke the mood whispering, "When was the last time we saw another car? I can't remember seeing anyone for quite a while now."

"I don't know. I hadn't thought about it. Some other headlights would sure be helpful. I can't believe we're on the main highway to Switzerland!"

"Do you think we should turn around?" he asked.

"Could we? What if we got stuck trying? You're right. There's nobody around!"

Then, suddenly, John was fighting the steering wheel. The white path of the road curved to the left, but the car kept going straight. He stomped on the brake, and we slid to a stop. He climbed out, no boots, of course, slamming his door behind him. I had no idea what he might be able to do. Neither did he. He circled the car, re-opened his door, and tugged on the wheel some more, but the wheels didn't turn. Next, I heard him kicking and kicking. Each kick was followed by a large "thud."

Climbing back in the car, he looked as white as the night, so I helped brush off the snow coating his hair and eyelashes.

Breathlessly, he said, "I hope that does it. The wheels were encased in ice. Cross your fingers while I try the steering."

Our faithful little Bug lurched over the ice chunks and took hold of the soft, but deepening snow. The wheels turned. We cheered.

In spite of the concentration needed to hold the car on the road, the magic of the glittering schneekristalls filled us with awe, and we proceeded again in reverent silence. Soon we sensed that the road was mostly heading downhill. The lower we drove, the lighter the snow fall, the easier the driving, and the brighter our mood.

Finally, John crowed, "Look, see, through there, a light."

Indeed, a pinpoint of light appeared well below us through the gauze of falling snow. We continued descending the mountainside as more lights peeped from behind rocks and trees. Ahead in the road each vehicle drove to the same spot, but then turned around and drove away. Finally, we neared a pair of headlights stopped in the oncoming lane and realized a sign, dark from our side, stood squarely in the middle of the road. It looked just like the one we had passed on the other side of the mountain. As John eased the car around it, I could get a good look in the other car's high beams: *Geschlossen*! Closed! The road was closed! We had just traversed a pass through the Alps on a road closed due to snow. Thank goodness for our new car. It might look and act like a beetle, not a cheetah like the Opel, but it got us through. And we had been too stupid to be afraid.

A king who feared wasps once decreed that they were abolished. As it happened, they did him no harm. But he was eventually stung to death by scorpions.
—Idries Shah, *Reflections* 1968

Crossing the Alps

20

Stood Up on Christmas (Eve?)

"How are we going to act around Peter?" John asked as he buttoned his white dress shirt which he hadn't worn for almost a year.

"I don't have a clue!" I mumbled from inside my Sunday-best dress, stuck over my face and shoulders, my arms straight above my head. John, realizing I was trapped, gave the thing a few tugs from the hem and I popped out above.

"Ooh, I didn't know that would be so tight," I gasped. "More holiday goodies around my middle than I thought."

"I don't know what else we can do but act like nothing ever happened."

"We can't exactly ask him for a translation of whatever he yelled at his mother."

"No. I guess it's just 'merry, merry' and 'jingle, jingle' and hope for the best," John concluded.

Frau Schaeffer hadn't set an exact time, just said she would call up the stairs for us when dinner was ready. We were ready by five o'clock. We didn't want to keep anyone waiting. Taking a cue from her fancy gray dress and stockings when we had invited her for a mere glass of wine, we dressed in our most festive holiday clothes, even shined our shoes. After all, one of Frau Schaeffer's sons-in-law was an American officer. Most importantly, it was

Christmas Eve, the beginning of the happiest, most blessed 24 hours of the entire year.

In Iowa we would be having our usual Christmas celebrations. For my family that would mean Dad reading the Christmas story from the Bible. Periodically he paused for a carol to match the text, such as "O Little Town of Bethlehem" or "Away in a Manger," which I would pound out on the piano while my family sang. Engrossed in the spirit, we all sang at the top of our lungs so the Lord would surely hear although none of us could carry a tune. Because we all outdid each other trying to find the perfect gifts for one another, the tree always looked buried in the surrounding presents. And then, Santa would come during the night. For years he brought a doll every Christmas because, of course, I had been a very good girl. Even though my brother and I were well beyond the Santa years, and now there was a son-in-law, too. Mom and Dad still treasured being Santa, and I still savored being their little girl at Christmas.

John's version of Christmas centered on his cousins. Growing up in a three-generation household with his grandparents, his family Christmas meant his aunts and uncles and cousins came from out of town for Christmas Eve, but after the celebration, the parents went home and the kids stayed with Grandma—for a week! His sister Jackie was the oldest, while he was the youngest. All six cousins tore through the two-story farmhouse plus attic racing from one card game or magic show rehearsal or batch of sugar cookies to the next. John's Grandma was a saint.

But, as newlyweds living in Germany, we not only had no family, but, also, we had no Christmas tree. We couldn't afford the lights, which being 220 volt, would have no use once we left Germany anyway. We took what few marks we did have to buy a German, candle-powered Christmas carousel as our substitute tree. It stood about 20 inches tall with three platforms of carved figures set amid palm trees: Mary, Joseph, and Baby Jesus huddled on the lowest tier; the three wise men with gifts, riding camels, traveled round and round in the middle; and at the top of the pyramid, the shepherds watched over their flock. In the base three lit candles provided enough warmth to make the tinker-toy-looking blades around the top slowly turn the carousel. We set it amid fresh pine boughs on the chest of drawers on our landing where it could be seen every time we used the stairs or went from one room to another. We decorated it by tying festive, foil-wrapped marzipan and liqueur-filled chocolates to the pine branches, at least better than popcorn and cranberries. Then we placed our few presents among the boughs. Unlike a tree, we would be able to take the carousel home with us for future Christmases. We were right! Forty-seven years later it still graces an end table near the tree every Christmas season. Our children referred to it as the Christmas go-round and now the grandchildren do the same although it stopped going around years ago.

On this Christmas Eve, we were excited to be part of a German family Christmas, learn more about German Christmas customs, and perhaps, who knew, get to know Peter at last. So, we sat primly trying not to wrinkle our clothes as we read and waited, prepared for the call to dinner whenever it came. By six o'clock we thought it strange that we didn't smell anything cooking. We always knew what was happening in Frau Schaeffer's kitchen as the often vinegary onion and cabbage fumes unfortunately ascended the open staircase without obstacle. At seven o'clock still nothing wafting our way. Neither were there any hearty sounds of a family gathering. "Not a creature was stirring." Wouldn't her family have driven to their mother's house on Christmas Eve? Yet our little VW bug sat all alone in the street out front.

By eight o'clock we were starving but had little on hand except some leftover crackers. I wanted to go find Frau Schaeffer, knocking on doors below. John was afraid we would humiliate her expecting dinner when she obviously had none. What on earth happened? Where was her own family? What were our own families back home doing without us? Were they as lonely as we were? So, we did nothing until late when we finally gave up and changed into our pajamas, ate a cold bowl of "un-cheery" Cheerios, and went to bed hungry and homesick. We felt stood up on Christmas Eve!

We began Christmas Day with those same blasted Cheerios, not my mother's cinnamon rolls made from her mother's recipe. It was some consolation that we would get to talk with my family on the phone later that afternoon, but I spent the morning trying not to cry. My family lived an ocean away. I would not see them on Christmas Day for the first time in my life, nor would they see me. They would be celebrating without me for the first time in 23 years. I couldn't decide who I felt worse for, them or me!

After breakfast John and I unwrapped our own gifts to each other. John had saved a few marks somehow for a Hummel figurine for me, and I had saved the coins from my grocery change for months for a German beer stein for him. After some lingering hugs of thanks, we indulged in a couple of our edible ornaments from the pine boughs as well as nibbling at the peanut brittle and fudge Mom had sent air mail. That was it. No morning filled with opening presents. No brunch with cinnamon rolls. No standing-rib roast dinner with butter-laden mashed potatoes and Mom's gravy oozing over every bite.

We dressed to leave for Christmas dinner with Louise and Nolan at their apartment. Since I had continued blubbering off-and-on all morning, I ducked back into the bathroom to patch my runny mascara and faced myself eye-to-eye in the mirror. I could not escape the realization that John and I had each other, and he was not celebrating alone or in Vietnam. If he had been sent to Nam, I would, indeed, be home with my own family. But, no, I was with him, where I belonged. We were married. I was a grown woman, not a child, and I was right where I most wanted and needed to be, beside my husband. I quickly patched my attitude and my eye makeup. I didn't know then that my hormones had good reason to be running amuck. We wouldn't find out the cause for another month, however.

We had a convivial, but sober, Christmas dinner at noon with our friends, spaghetti and meat balls, Louise's specialty learned from her Italian next-door neighbor back in Massachusetts. She didn't measure the oregano or basil, piling it in the palm of her hand until it looked the right size. After stirring the spices into the ground beef, she tasted the raw meat. Not something I'd seen in Iowa, but the result, once cooked, tasted far different than the canned Chef Boyardee my mother gave us when Dad traveled out of town on business. We talked about our New Year's plans for our trip to Amsterdam. We hoped to see windmills and skaters on the canals and the Anne Frank house. After a few hands of cards next to their Christmas tree, Nolan had to leave for an evening shift of street duty, the reason for the sobriety. We hugged each other and group-hugged some more with lots of wishes for a "Merry Christmas" as we left.

Then John and I headed to the Post Office in downtown Mannheim. On Christmas Day, you may be asking? Wouldn't it be closed? The Post Office stayed open even on Christmas Day as that was the only place where you could make a transatlantic telephone call. We had had to book the call a week earlier for today at 16:00 or four o'clock in the afternoon which would be nine o'clock in the morning in Iowa. We signed in at the desk and waited on the hard, wooden benches opposite the row of telephone booths lining the side wall. Soon the clerk called, "Powoool, *vier*." We recognized our name from Frau Schaeffer's pronunciation and entered booth four. The phone rang, I grabbed the receiver knowing we had only three minutes. I could hear my father, slurping coffee, undoubtedly to wash down his cinnamon roll. Mom tried to sound joyous, but as her voice caught, I could tell she fought the tears. I have no idea what we talked about for three minutes, nothing important, but hearing the voices was what mattered.

We arrived home to our apartment around dark to find the house lit up ironically like the proverbial Christmas tree, and, sure enough, several cars were parked in front, including the big Chrysler that belonged to Frau Schaeffer's American son-in-law. When we opened the front door, the strong smell of roasting meat escaped. The sounds of conversation, laughter, and silverware clinking on china came from behind the dining room door, closed as usual to preserve the warmth. We quietly tip-toed upstairs not knowing what to make of the situation, let alone what to do about it.

"Should we go down and knock on the dining room door?" I asked.

"Lord, no. What if she didn't mean to include us?" John retorted.

"You don't suppose she meant to invite us for dinner on Christmas *Day*?" I asked.

"I'm sure she said Christmas *Eve*," he replied emphatically. "Isn't that what you thought she said?"

"Yes, that's what I heard. You don't suppose the family changed it to Christmas Day and she forgot to tell us? We'd better go down and straighten it out, apologize, whatever," I insisted.

"We can't go down there. We've already eaten. I couldn't eat another thing and that would be an insult, too," he argued turning away from me.

"I know!" I exclaimed. "I bet she doesn't understand that in English Christmas Eve is the night before Christmas. She probably thinks English for Christmas is Christmas Eve."

"Geez, if that's the case . . . she's so proud of her English . . . how can we tell her she messed this up because of her English?" he objected pacing the kitchen floor.

"We can't let her think we blew off her invitation. I could never look her in the eye again. Better that she knows it's a language problem than think we didn't bother to show up on Christmas," I pleaded.

"Absolutely not. I won't go. I won't tell that proud woman she doesn't know how to say Christmas!" John fired back.

A marital disagreement: the perfect ending to our perfect Christmas!

We seemed angry with each other, but with many years perspective, I can appreciate our frustration with a situation we had no idea how to resolve. As he has put it himself, "We don't really fight, but sometimes we have different needs." I always want to rush in and tackle things head on, like a bull, which makes him, being more reserved, quite uncomfortable.

Several days later when I encountered Frau Schaeffer on the stairs, she asked, "Vhere vere you on Christmas Eve?" Yes, she said, Christmas *Eve*, not where were you on Christmas? I insisted we were at home, but in her heavy German accent she replied breathily, "But ve call for you. My son knock on your doors. I invite you to dinner . . . vith my family. Your car vas not in front of house."

I so wanted to ask her about her definition of Christmas Eve, but knowing how strongly John felt, I merely replied, "We were home all evening on Christmas Eve, the night before Christmas. On Christmas Day, during the day, we went to our friends, but not on Christmas Eve, the night before Christmas, we were at home."

She shrugged her shoulders and rolled her eyes, her typical expression. She never showed any sign that she figured it out. Probably, just like us, she felt stood up on Christmas Eve.

✛

Eva's Christmas Goodies

◆————◆

Frohes Neues Jahr

December 31,1969: On the Billboard Year End Top 100, the songs "Aquarius" and "Hair" from the Broadway musical Hair *finish in 2nd and 13th positions respectively for the year 1969.*

December 31, 1969: US troop levels in Vietnam reach 475,200 Americans, 11,780 die.

"Watch out! Here comes another one," John yelled as he covered my head with his arms.

"This is insane, totally insane," I stammered from his arm pit. I clung to him as the fireworks exploded, whizzing around us, and I remembered that dreadful Fourth of July when I was six.

In 1952 Mom and Dad had hosted a large party where all the guests brought fireworks for the celebration. Before dark all of us kids spent much of the party in anticipation around the collection displayed on a card table, sorting and counting the pinwheels, the waterfalls, the skyrockets, the Roman candles, the comets, the snakes, and the sparklers. After dinner, as dark approached, my dad and the other men began to light them one at a time on the far side of the yard, but one rained a tiny spark onto that table. In minutes it was more like Doomsday than Independence Day. As the pinwheels caught they spun off the table in all directions, followed by rockets zooming up or down or sideways. Roman candles sprouted like it was Dante's inferno. I remember running around the house and trying to bury myself underneath the evergreen shrubs in the front yard, but, of course, some of the errant fireworks made it over our one-story, ranch-style house as if chasing me. For years those rockets screamed over me again and again in my nightmares, and I dreaded the Fourth of July worse than a shot in the fanny. Now here they were again as we stood outside near Bonn, West Germany, on New Year's Eve.

That afternoon we had driven toward Bonn from Mannheim. When we saw a brightly lit *Gasthaus,* a neighborhood pub with guest rooms, on the outskirts of town, John stopped in front, and I was dispatched to use my feeble German to inquire about an upstairs room for the night. A gentleman in a suit greeted me in the entry.

"*Haben Sie ein Doppelzimmer frei?*" I inquired.

"*Ja, wir haben.*"

"*Wie viel kostet das?*"

"*Zwanzig Mark.*"

"*Sehr gut,*" I responded nodding my acceptance. The price for a double room for one night, around $5, was exactly what *Frommers* predicted in our copy of his latest edition of *Europe on $5 a Day.* I waved out the door for John to join me with the luggage.

The proprietor motioned for us to be seated while he ran off up the stairs. By the time he returned 10 minutes later, we had become worried. He then showed us up to the room with the German double bed, two twins pushed together, both covered by an overstuffed down comforter that made your inner child want to dive in, grab your pillow, and start exuberantly pummeling your bedmate.

He pointed out the shared bathroom down the hall, which we had expected at that price. Both were as immaculate as if they had just been cleaned by my German mother, who believed that cleanliness was, indeed, next to godliness. Later when we happened to open the top dresser drawer exposing the various hairpins, combs, and a hairbrush tangled with gray hair, we knew we were in what must usually serve as Grandma's room. This family needed the twenty marks as most German families did. We wondered where Grandma was sleeping tonight?

Once freshened, we went downstairs for our own holiday dinner. In the restaurant and bar section on the main floor, German couples, mostly middle-aged or older, were already gathering for their holiday night out: a dinner of multiple courses that they would linger over until midnight. The evening started quietly and formally as we had learned to expect from the Germans. They chatted in reserved voices with others at their table. We knew the patrons would be neighbors who could walk to their local gasthaus, as they did many evenings for *Weisswein* or *Bier,* white wine or beer, followed by some card-playing. This community tradition had existed for centuries in Europe, and the advent of television had not extinguished it yet. Tonight, they had dressed up, however, and would stay into the New Year.

We felt a bit conspicuous being youngsters and strangers, but no one seemed to mind. As others finished their meals, they brought out their decks of cards and the conversation became more animated with the hurrahs of winners slapping their trump on the cards played by the groaning losers. Just before midnight everyone stood up and moved toward the door. We didn't know what to do.

Did they leave at midnight before the New Year? We still had some wine left for a toast and wanted to stay. Seeing our confusion, someone motioned for us to come, too. No one had put on a coat, so we decided they were going outside for the arrival of 1970. We followed the throng. Once outside, they counted down through the last minute of the old year beginning with 60: *"Sechzig, neunundfünfzig, achtundfünfzig . . . drei, zwei, eins."* Everyone yelled together, *"Frohes neues Jahr*!!!!" And then the blankety-blank fireworks began. Like home, everyone brought some to contribute, but they each ignited their own from wherever they stood in the crowd. They all exuded holiday spirit, German *Gemütlichkeit*. What happened to the quiet we had experienced in our own neighborhood, the quiet that made us feel too boisterous when we conversed with friends while walking them to their car at the end of an evening? For me it was terror.

John hustled me inside, so I had some time to compose myself before the rest returned to their tables. Once everyone was in, the two couples seated by the window got up and started around the room moving from one table to another, shaking hands, grinning broadly, and repeating, "Frohes neues Jahr," the *J* pronounced like a *Y* in English. So here they came, right to our table.

We rose and extended our hands to theirs, "Fro new Jahr," John stumbled.

A motherly woman helped him, pronouncing each word, "Fro-hes-neu-es-Jahr."

"Frohes neues Jahr," he responded rhythmically accenting the first syllable on "Frohes" and "neues" and punching the "Jahr" at the end. As each table filed past,

160

we shook many hands and got a lot of practice saying Happy New Year in German. Some even tried their English on us, but we tried to honor them by replying in their language. Feeling accepted, we made our circuit as well to show our appreciation for their warm and welcoming inclusion. And then the bartender brought around schnapps on the house for everybody. Who would have thought during the fireworks that the evening could turn so dramatically?

The next day, New Year's Day, instead of watching the Rose Bowl Parade and football games, we headed our gray Bug toward Amsterdam via Cologne and its famous Cathedral. The Cologne Cathedral, under construction from the 13th to the 19th century, was built to house the relics of the Magi Kings given to the archbishopric in Cologne in 1164. You know the Magi, the ones who brought gold, frankincense, and myrrh to the newborn Jesus. The gray stone shrine, all pointed arches, gables, and windows, mounting in line with the spires over 500 feet above, matched the damp gray winter clouds and the damp gray of the adjacent Rhine River lapping at the quay. My feet quickly numbed as the cold of the stones beneath permeated through my shoes before we even made it to the door. Once inside, the sheer size and sweep of the nave overwhelmed us. A Mass was in progress, so we had to be satisfied with that brief peek, probably a good thing in the cold, no central heating in cathedrals, but we knew we must return in the summer.

Heading on toward Amsterdam, we admired the ancient, picture-postcard windmills all along the route.

"Those are too cute. Bet they were planted by AAA just to attract tourists," John exclaimed.

"Hey, there's another one. Stop. I've got to get a picture . . . we've got to share these with our folks! Can't you stop on the shoulder?" I begged.

"No. You know it's illegal on the Autobahn, or the *Autosnelweg,* whatever they call this Dutch highway. You want me to get arrested?" Over his own objections, he slowed and pulled onto the shoulder at the next windmill, but he hadn't forgiven me by the time he had to come up with the next cartoon to send home. In reality the only police car was in John's paranoid imagination.

Pat Gets the Picture

Once in Amsterdam we used our Frommers to find a cute little room nestled in the gables, up many skinny, winding stairs, in a narrow canal house. The view from our single dormer window consisted of the numerous rooflines behind the house, more like a cubist painting, intersecting planes and angles in various textures and shades of terra cotta, oozing with "quaint." We wished we had ice skates as we envied the locals who skimmed by on the canals rather than plodding down the cold streets.

I would like to write about the happy times eating on the balcony of the famous Five Flies restaurant where we first smelled marijuana, oohing over Rembrandts and aahing over Van Goghs, imbibing free beer and cheese at the Heineken factory, but we mainly came to see the Anne Frank house. We waited almost an hour in line, in January, more numb feet. But once inside, behind the movable bookcase, we realized how small a price we had paid. During World War II two Jewish families plus a dentist friend, eight people, had hid in the cramped apartment behind that bookcase for over two years before being detected by the Nazis in August 1944.

Everyone our age growing up in America in the fifties and sixties knew Anne Frank. A friend of the family had found her diary in the family's belongings after the Gestapo discovered their hiding place and took them away to a concentration camp. The diary, detailing the experience of her family while hiding in Amsterdam, had been published in English in the US in 1952. Translated into over 60 languages, it became an international bestseller. By 1955 it had been adapted into a play winning the Pulitzer Prize for Drama. It became a movie in 1959, eventually chosen for the American Film Institute's list

100 Years . . . 100 Cheers, the 100 most inspiring films ever. John and I had both read the book and seen the movie. In the camps Anne and her sister died of typhus, and their mother died of starvation. Only one of the eight, Anne's father, Otto Frank, survived the death camps and the war.

Years later I would teach her diary in middle school English. I would begin with a black and white slide show on Nazi persecution of the Jews in World War II including the concentration camps. The first slide, against a somber black background, bore five words, all caps, in white block type:

IT MUST
NEVER
HAPPEN AGAIN!

I always felt I had a mission. I would recap my experience of sliding behind the movable bookcase into a garret, more labyrinthine, but otherwise not unlike the one I lived in myself in Europe. But only two people lived in our garret, and we could walk outside any time we wanted. While we didn't have extra money, couldn't waste extra pennies on extraneous items such as chewing gum, we had turkey at Thanksgiving and plenty of Riesling wine and German beer. The dramatic irony of reading Anne's words made a deep impression on my students. She wanted to be a writer when she grew up, yet the reader knew her coming fate, that she would not grow up. She wrote about how the families padded around silently during the day so the factory workers below couldn't hear them, and without ever feeling a fresh breeze or sunshine warming their faces, they could only watch the seasons pass through their attic windows. They shared their meager food supplies available only with falsified ration books depending on Mr. Frank's trusted employees for all needs. Yet, Anne wrote in her diary, "It's difficult in times like these: ideals, dreams and cherished hopes rise within us, only to be crushed by grim reality. It's a wonder I haven't abandoned all my ideals, they seem so absurd and impractical. Yet I cling to them because I still believe, in spite of everything, that people are truly good at heart."

. . . the US restricted immigration in the name of protecting national security. A suspicion of those who were different, Anti-Semitism and xenophobia played a part. Otto Frank had powerful friends in the US, including Nathan Straus, the son of an owner of Macy's. Straus agreed to pay thousands of dollars to help secure visas and documents, but it was not enough.

—Margot Adler, *All Things Considered,*

National Public Radio 2007

Reminding ourselves that being human also means being inhuman is important simply because it is so easy to forget our inhumanity or to displace it onto others. . . . If we do not recognize our capacity to victimize, then it would be difficult for us to prevent the victimization carried out on our behalf, or which we do ourselves.

—Viet Thanh Nguyen,

Nothing Ever Dies 2016

Dear Charley,

I am forced to look out for emigration and as far as I can see USA is the only country we could go to. Perhaps you remember that we have two girls. It is for the sake of the children mainly that we have to care for.

—Otto Frank April 30, 1941

22

◆━━━━◆

Pregnant

February 18, 1970: Five of the Chicago 7, young leaders of the student protesters at the 1968 Democratic Convention, are found guilty of violating the Anti-Riot Act of 1968.

March 26, 1970: Woodstock, *a documentary film chronicling the legendary* Woodstock Music and Art Festival *held near Bethel, New York, in August 1969, is released.*

March 1970: The movie version of M*A*S*H is released in the US. The movie portrays two unorthodox army doctors stationed at a Korean War field hospital. Between surgeries they use screwball humor to survive the horrors of war under the leadership of a gung-ho career officer.

April 11–17, 1970: The Apollo 13 *mission, intending to make the third moon landing, aborts after two oxygen tanks explode forcing makeshift repairs. In spite of numerous difficulties and hardships, the flight returns safely to Earth.*

January 1969–April, 1970: The Senate Permanent Subcommittee on Investigations finds that the US sustained 4,330 bombings during the period. After analysis of the civil disturbances, Dr John P Spiegel, director of Brandeis University's Lemberg Center for the Study of Violence, states: "... they were motivated by the ineffectiveness of peaceful protests against the war."

The white curtains surrounding my hospital bed parted. Finally. John had arrived. He gasped involuntarily when he saw me. One glance at his face told me what I must look like curled up in a tight ball, ironically, a fetal position. I knew I lay in a puddle of my own sweat, hair undoubtedly lank, face pale, eyes glazed, my only focus the relentless pain in my belly, not the intermittent contractions of labor, but constant, wrenching pain as though some beast was tearing me apart from the inside out. John took my hand in his, and with his other hand stroked my arm gently but deliberately. I struggled to make his touch my new focus.

"It's seven o'clock," he whispered. "They called the company just after lunch, and Sarge let Larson drive me down here, but then they wouldn't let me see you until visiting hours."

I tried to answer, but nothing came out.

"Oh, Hon," he murmured and bent closer. "No one will tell me anything. What's going on?"

I muttered something unintelligible, and he leaned his ear close to my mouth. I felt a tear drop onto my cheek. With all my might I tried again. "I dunno'. Nurse says, 'Ask doctor.' But I haven't seen a doctor."

"Oh, Pat. I saw our Bug in the parking lot, but how did you make it . . . alone?"

"Had to. Remember . . . Doc said . . . if spotting . . . heavy . . . Heidelberg Hospital," I muttered breathlessly before collapsing. He knew I couldn't call him at the company. He was "unaccompanied." I was unauthorized.

An hour later, visiting was over, and the nurse forced him to leave me, as harsh for him as it was for me. We had no idea what was happening to me, something to do with being pregnant, but beyond that, no idea. The pain kept me prostrate. I knew from inside my curtained cocoon that I was in a ward with other mothers as I could hear babies crying, nurses coming and going, bringing babies from the nursery for feedings. Growing up in the fifties and early sixties was a time when women shrouded their reproductive functions in strictest secrecy. For another two hours, I lay in this state, barely conscious. Suddenly, the pain ended abruptly as I felt a rush of fluid between my legs. I tried to look at what lay on the sheets, but reflexively jerked away as the pinkish puddle contained a tiny mass that looked to me more like a tadpole than a human.

Several weeks before this, we had found out I was two months pregnant. Today our kids would say, "We were pregnant," but I was the one with morning sickness. We had written joyous letters to our parents and received thrilled replies. Louise taught me to knit, so I was immersed in attempting to create a hooded baby sack with drawstring closure. Yellow, because before ultra sounds were used, we had no idea whether our baby would be a boy or a girl.

But then, just as the morning sickness was going away, I had started spotting, just a little pink occasionally in my panties. The army doc said that was common, not to worry unless it became heavy red blood. In that case I was to get myself to the Heidelberg Hospital immediately, which made sense when you were bleeding. So, I had done that.

Finally, once I was no longer in pain and afraid for my life, a doctor appeared. With a clipboard in hand, he announced, "You've had a spontaneous abortion."

"What's that?" I blurted.

He explained, "It's nature's way of eliminating babies that may be malformed, not developing properly. It happens fairly frequently . . . about 10-20% of women have their pregnancies end this way . . . usually during the first three months. Actually, you're lucky. You've been saved from having to take care of an abnormal child, undoubtedly with major health issues."

I had never heard of a *spontaneous abortion*. And I definitely didn't feel lucky.

He scheduled me for a D&C the next day, a routine surgery to make sure that no tissue remained in my uterus that could cause infection. Of course, any visitation with John was not in his plan. The next morning I came out of the anesthesia on a gurney being wheeled down the hall. I started gagging and couldn't breathe. Panicked, I began thrashing around wildly. Someone quickly pulled something out of my throat. Later, I found out it was a rubber airway used in the operating room to keep a patient's tongue from blocking their throat. Because of the gag reflex, it is only to be used under anesthesia. Surprise, surprise. I was awake! Hello?

Later that day another young wife in pain was admitted on the ward to the bed next to mine. I could tell after her husband's visit, not much privacy in adjacent beds even with the curtains drawn, that they were experiencing what we had gone through the night before. Now I could get out of bed, so I went to her and held her hand. I'll never forget her large, round eyes wild with the pain. She had no idea, either, that she was having a "spontaneous abortion."

"What's going on? What's happening to me?" she moaned frantically.

I talked to her softly repeating what the doctor had told me, skipping the part about being lucky. I assured her the pain would stop and stayed with her for several hours that night until, she, too, lost her baby. I might have been a stranger, but she wasn't alone.

> Is it useful to feel fear, because it prepares you for nasty events, or is it useless, because nasty events will occur whether you are frightened or not?
> —Lemony Snicket,
> *The Wide Window* 2000

23

———◆———

Students or Military?

April 30, 1970: President Nixon announces the invasion of Cambodia requiring an additional draft of 150,000 troops. This provokes massive student protests across the country.

May 4, 1970: Following the torching of the ROTC building at Kent State University, the Ohio National Guard shoots into a crowd of unarmed students killing four and wounding nine.

May 9, 1970: Over 100,000 demonstrators march in Washington, DC, smashing windows, slashing tires, dragging parked cars into intersections, and throwing box springs off overpasses onto traffic below. President Nixon is taken to Camp David for two days for his own protection.

May 15, 1970: Neil Young's song "Ohio," in response to Kent State, is banned on many radio stations. When Crosby, Stills, Nash & Young finished the recording in the studio, David Crosby cried.

May 1970: Over four million students participate in the only nationwide student strike in US history. They disrupt over 450 college and university campuses with non-violent and violent demonstrations forcing many schools to close prematurely for the year.

After the miscarriage, we needed some fun adventures, so we pointed our scummy Bug toward England,

Belgium, and France, leaving behind the Armed Forces Radio, the *Stars and Stripes* newspaper, and the APO mail service from home. The first evening back in Mannheim, John returned from work racing up the stairs two at a time. He held the stack of mail that had accumulated during our two-week absence.

"Pat, Pat," he yelled, oblivious to disturbing Frau Schaeffer, very uncharacteristic. He waved an envelope in the air. "The Kleins are coming. Mary and Steve are coming to Mannheim, almost any day they could be here."

John shoved the letter into my hands, and I eagerly read. Mary wrote that Steve had allowed himself to be arrested at a non-violent demonstration in Iowa City protesting the Kent State shootings.

"Steve has been in jail!" I gulped in disbelief. She also reported destruction on campus, especially window smashing and looting at Iowa Book and Supply, known as Iowa BS by the students forced to pay monopolistic textbook prices.

I started reading Mary's letter aloud: "The U has closed, no finals, no graduation ceremony. Our diplomas came in the mail yesterday."

I looked at John. "How can that be? I heard something on the Armed Forces Radio today about an investigation following the shootings at Kent State, but I-I didn't know what they were talking about," I stammered. "Do you know?"

"What shootings? What's happened while we've been gone?" he fired back rifling through the stack of mail until he found our *Time* magazine. Together we paged wildly through the images. We found the iconic photograph of a student lying dead on the ground, with another, a hysterical girl, kneeling over him, arms flailing in the air. It won the Pulitzer. Other photos showed kneeling National Guardsmen firing into the college crowd. Thus, we found out about the student deaths at Kent State.

Had the world turned upside down? We didn't support the war, but we didn't support violence either, from police and guardsmen or from protesting students. The ends still did not justify any means. Philosophically, we actually aligned with the Beatles, who took a lot of guff from the militant protest movement after the release of their song "Revolution" which revealed their opposition to violence with the lyrics "But when you talk about destruction don't you know that you can count me out." It didn't make sense, then or now, to end the violence of the war through more violence. And now there was this horror, Kent State, the tables turned, both protestors and innocent by-standers dead. Yes, students at Kent State had set the ROTC building on fire, but the guilty parties were not the ones shot. Even if they had been, they deserved a trial, not a summary execution. And worse, two of the four dead were not protesters. They were students killed by stray bullets while walking to class.

Also troubling for us, the students were throwing rocks at the National Guard. The troops should somehow be able to protect themselves, but absolutely not by shooting at kids armed only with rocks. What if John had been one of those troops? Could he be injured? The MPs didn't have riot gear. Could he have heard others shooting, thought there was a sniper, as some guardsmen claimed, and fired himself? It's a decision made in an instant, in less than a heartbeat, a decision that could alter lives, someone else's and your own. Was he really trained for that? Could anyone really be trained for that? What if the 537th MP Company were ever called upon to police German student demonstrations against the war? Only days after Kent State, Crosby, Stills, Young & Nash recorded "Ohio," an often-banned song warning "Nixon's coming" and referring to the guardsmen as "tin soldiers." As an MP, John could be one of those tin soldiers. Here was something more to fear. I caught a glimpse of the Elephant smiling out at me from under the bed. Bottom line: at heart were we students or were we military?

> I am a spy . . . a man of two faces. Perhaps not surprisingly, I am also a man of two minds, . . . able to see any issue from both sides.
>
> —Viet Thanh Nguyen,
The Sympathizer 2016

Amidst the schizophrenia caused by the anguish of Kent State and the excitement of seeing the Kleins soon, we discovered that the movie *M*A*S*H* had finally arrived at the Armed Forces theaters. The line to buy our 10 cent tickets wrapped around the red brick building, and we, having decided to go at the last minute, found ourselves almost at the end. That was fine with me. I always felt so conspicuous, sometimes being the only female in the theater. Most of the audience at these movies, mainly draftees like John, couldn't help staring at a girl from home. We both remember that we had to sit in the only seats left in the front row, on the far right side. The solid-wood, fold-down seats, antiques from World War II, creaked as we sat down forcing us to carefully test whether they would hold before settling in.

The film's anti-army hijinks took place in a Mobile Army Surgical Hospital (MASH) unit during the Korean War, a thinly-veiled disguise for Vietnam. Right away we identified with the company clerk from Iowa, Corporal O'Reilly, nick-named Radar, for his quiet and uncanny ability to handle a situation before his boss, Colonel Blake, could figure it out. When two newly-drafted surgeons, Hawkeye Pierce and Trapper John McIntyre, arrive at the company in a stolen jeep, unassuming Radar, dressed in an over-sized white T-shirt and baggy fatigue pants, demonstrates his mental acuity:

> RADAR. Gentlemen, I'm Corporal O'Reilly, they call me Radar. You'll be staying in Major Burns' tent. I'll take your things over there now.
> COLONEL BLAKE. Get everything out of the Jeep...
> RADAR, *while Blake continues speaking.* Don't worry about the Jeep. I'll change the numbers.
> COLONEL BLAKE. . . . All their duffel bags, all their gear. . . Oh, and change the numbers on that Jeep.

Did we identify with Radar because he was from Iowa? That wasn't all. John had worked for months as Morning Report Clerk, no longer on street duty. Initially street duty had held the allure of excitement, frankly because it was so hard to imagine John, a guy who had never been in a fist fight, as a cop, a tough guy. The reality proved boring. Much of the time street duty consisted of driving around for eight hours with nothing to do. When something did happen, the most common calls came for domestic disturbances in Benjamin Franklin Village, the army housing for accompanied troops. Who would want to deal with a husband and wife throwing plates or punches at each other? And once the newness of wearing a .45 on his hip wore off, the reality that he might someday actually have to use it overshadowed any glamor.

Some officer, knowing John was a college boy, asked him if he knew how to type. Desperate to be off the rotating shifts that left his body habitually sleep-deprived, he eagerly puffed his typing skills. He didn't volunteer that he hadn't had a keyboarding class or that his wife, back when she was his head-over-heels fiancée, had typed all of his papers for the last year and a half of his college career.

As Morning Report Clerk, he had to be on duty well before daylight in order to produce the Morning Report which had to be at headquarters by the time the Colonel arrived. The report detailed all of the unit's personnel changes effective that day and was tabulated to determine troop strength at each administrative level. Army regulations stated that morning reports could not have over a specified number of typing errors, so it had to be typed over and over and over until the clerk produced a copy with only an allowable number of corrections. And it had to be done on a firm deadline. With John's hunt-and-peck at under 35 words per minute, he killed some trees and, being the army, undoubtedly fouled the air with some expletives. This duty had been temporary, he could be returned to street patrol on anyone's whim. Just another uncertainty. Radar was our hero; however, Radar still slept with his Teddy bear. Happily, I served that function for John.

However, for most of the audience, the movie centered around the conflict between Hawkeye and Trapper John versus the gung-ho "lifers," career officers, Major Frank Burns, a less than competent army surgeon, and his accomplice Major "Hot Lips" O'Hoolihan, the head nurse. In various gags Hawkeye and Trapper John managed to make fools of the lifers and their army regulations providing sweet release for the audience. But then the bombshell dropped in this scene:

> HOT LIPS O'HOOLIHAN, *referring to Hawkeye*. I wonder how a degenerated person like that could have reached a position of responsibility in the Army Medical Corps?
>
> FATHER MULCAHY, *looking up from his Bible*. He was drafted.

Those words unleashed bedlam, everyone on their feet, shouting, whistling, pounding on each other. A bunch of guys behind us jumped onto the rickety wooden seats dancing on the arms and backs, stomping and whooping, until the wood gave way delivering the revelers to the floor in a heap of hysterical, guffawing bodies amid splintered wood. Bumps and bruises, yes, but nobody cared. Laughter heals!

✠

There was only one catch and that was Catch-22, which specified that a concern for one's own safety in the face of dangers that were real and immediate was the process of a rational mind. Orr was crazy and could be grounded. . . . Orr would be crazy to fly more missions and sane if he didn't, but if he was sane, he had to fly them. If he flew them, he was crazy and didn't have to; but if he didn't want to, he was sane and had to. . . .

"That's some catch, that Catch-22," he [Yossarian] observed.

"It's the best there is," Doc Daneeka agreed.

—Catch-22,

Joseph Heller 1961

Laughter is poison to fear.

—George RR Martin,
A Game of Thrones 1996

24

Flower Children

Now we awaited the arrival any day of Mary and Steve. Mary, a sorority sister two-years younger than myself, had tended the guest book at our wedding while Steve, a fine arts major in photography, took informal pictures for our album. Because we had been traveling, by the time we received their letter, they had already left for Germany. They didn't know exactly when they would get to Mannheim, soon after they picked up the VW Camper they had ordered in Hamburg. And they didn't know our apartment address, only our mailing address at the 537th MP Company in Turley Barracks. They figured they could find Turley Barracks and the 537th MP Company and ask for John.

They never knew how nervous that made him. Military lifers, his bosses in a system that demanded following orders, found hippies a serious challenge to their military worldview. Were our friends hippies? We had no idea what to expect. Mary had always had straight, waist-length, blonde hair, a natural flower child. Steve's hair, wavy and curly, had been trimmed close to his head, but would he have long hair now? Would he have a beard? Sometimes I puzzled over what difference hair made? How had hair become the symbol of the divisiveness in our country: the closely trimmed military supporters versus the bearded, long-haired hippies? Since when did hair indicate what was wrong and what was right? Check out a picture of the Founding Fathers. They didn't wear crew cuts; they wore their hair pulled back into ponytails at the nape of their necks. No one debated their patriotism! At other times I realized that having long hair and a beard was a conscious choice, a protest statement in opposition to the military crew cuts. We, at any rate, would be thrilled to see Mary and Steve with any amount of hair, but, if they looked like hippies, John fretted about any fallout from the lifers who saw him with them.

Indeed, the very next afternoon, the Kleins showed up at Turley Barracks when John was on desk duty, just before his quitting time, so they could follow him home. They made serious fun of all the shaven faces and shorn locks they'd seen there. Mary did have a hippie-style headband around her head and across her forehead like a halo holding her cascading golden hair in place, and Steve's blue eyes glittered from behind his mass of kinky beard and curly, unruly hair, with his cuddly-bear persona still escaping from underneath.

After unloading the camper, Steve came to the kitchen with an insulated travel pouch saying, "Hey, Pat. Can I keep this in your frig? It's my allergy kit. I have to give myself shots, and the stuff 's supposed to stay cold."

"Sure," I replied taking his pouch and moving the eggs to make room for it. "That's a bummer. You really give yourself shots?"

"Yea, but I don't mind. That's why I'm going to grad school in the fall instead of basic training."

"Whadda' ya mean? What do allergies have to do with the draft?"

Mary joined us taking a seat at the kitchen table while John was busy opening a bottle of Riesling and pouring it into four of our traditional German wine glasses, not stemmed, but supported on green rippling pedestal bases.

We quickly raised our glasses in a toast, more of a salute. "To our Alma Mater, the U of Iowa," Steve crowed.

"To the U of I," we yelled in unison clinking our glasses.

"So, Steve," John asked frowning, "what *do* allergies have to do with the draft?"

"Well, man, a lot of Iowa City docs are now against the war, too, so they hold free screening clinics to help guys find anything they can use for a 4-F to get out of the draft."

"Shee-it," John said pronouncing the word in two syllables like all the southern guys did at Fort Gordon. "So, I went to this doc the spring before I was drafted," he continued, "orthopedic, cuz my back goes out, an old trampoline accident in gym class. When it goes, it makes me walk around like Grandpa McCoy. My folks always took me to a chiropractor, so I didn't have any records from a doc. So, when this guy realized I was graduating and would be 1-A, he figured I was trying to make up an injury. He gave me an ear full about God and country and kicked me out of his office. Turns out he was on the local draft board."

"Whoops!" Mary exclaimed. "Now . . . when a guy gets his notice to report for a physical, he just goes to the clinic first. That's how Steve found out about his allergies."

"What a difference two years can make!" John exhaled through his teeth. Ironically, John has suffered from allergies to grasses virtually all of his adult life. Recently, he tested moderately to extremely allergic to all 29 items on the test. Timing is, indeed, everything.

182

Over the next few days more than a few bottles of local beer and Riesling wine disappeared as we sat around that table catching up on news from home, both personal and political. We also shared our local knowledge, tricks like buying a "flippy" or flip-top beer from a vending machine or keeping a wine bottle because it was refundable. We introduced them to the weisswurst grilled by street vendors and sold with brotchen which they loved like we did. We took them to buy the juicy roast chicken to-go at the chicken place. Every town had one. They were chagrined they couldn't afford Coca-Cola, a luxury item in Germany, but we could buy them a somewhat more affordable case at the Commissary. During the day, completely sober, we gave them a crash course, poor pun, in road signs as we shared nearby sights and pointed out helpful information like how to distinguish parking permitted from parking prohibited.

As John began a few days off on an unbearably hot and sultry evening in our third-floor apartment, we all decided the camper was stocked and ready for its maiden voyage. John had slept in a tent in his backyard on the farm, and of course, had professional camping experience courtesy of the US Army, but I had never been camping before, so this was high adventure. We chose the *Schwarzwald* or Black Forest for our destination. It sounded cool and shady. We didn't know about the mountains there. Packing the camper, we had no such thing in our apartment as American blankets, and we rejected the down comforter from our bed, way too bulky to fit in the camper van. Laughingly, John tossed in his army sleeping bag rated to below zero. We couldn't possibly need that, but it was compact!

The Kleins had a guidebook to camping spots, so we chose the most scenic-sounding campground and headed south down the Rhine Valley, at first on the Autobahn to the spa town of Baden-Baden, and then on the backroads past vineyards and orchards lined up neatly in rows. The winding crest road took us past cows wearing bells idling in the greenest of green pastures, through half-timbered villages, and to astonishing viewpoints, all the time gaining altitude. Our campground in the Allerheiligen area proved to be a mountain glade dotted with wildflowers next to a stream and surrounded by forest so thick it was, yes, black. We tucked flowers behind our ears, scrambled over rocks around the waterfall, and dared each other to see who could keep their bare feet in the rushing water, recently snowmelt, the longest.

Above the falls church ruins provided the penultimate symbol. After 700 years a roofed entrance remained intact leading into an open-ceilinged nave with only the bluebird-blue heavens above. Steve attempted to capture the spirituality of the place taking photos from every angle, through every window, from the ground, and from the top of anything he could scramble up. Under that sky, it was easy to "Imagine all the people living life in peace" as John Lennon did in his song "Imagine." How could a human being feel more in tune with the maker of the universe?

Back in the real world, the camper also proved to be a marvel, a marvel of German engineering, compact, yet complete. Steve demonstrated "popping the top." *Voila!*

You could stand up! Next, he flipped over the back seat. *Voila!* You could wash your hands and store your food in an ice box! He flipped another seat. *Voila!* You had a double bed extending the width of the van. Mary and I got the bed, Steve would take the hammock above, and John was supposed to be on a single mattress fitted over the top of the kitchen counter, sink, and ice box. At bed time John, the smart one, announced he would sleep on top of his GI sleeping bag outside under the porch awning. Mary and I bedded down, fully dressed for warmth, our jackets around our shoulders for covers. Steve swung precariously above us in the hammock. Surrounded by the cold on all sides, he tossed and turned. I lay awake sure that he would come crashing down upon us, all 200 pounds of him, at any moment. And it got colder. Our steamy apartment sounded great!

Finally, Steve had had enough. He came down from the hammock, dug out their only bedding, a "space" blanket, a spinoff of the American space program made of metal and hugely insulating, best described as thick aluminum foil, but too stiff to wrap around oneself. I had never heard of such a thing.

Steve climbed in on the other side of Mary to sleep with us in the double bed. The space blanket was only as wide as the bed, so it laid on top of us leaving nothing to tuck in around our sides or shoulders. From the waist down, squished between Mary and the camper, sealed with the space blanket on top, my body sweat profusely, droplets rolling between my legs. However, around my shoulders and down my back, the fresh mountain air rushed right in under the space blanket. I could feel the goosebumps popping up on my arms. I was a stew below the waist and an ice cube above.

Finally, just before dawn, I had had enough, too. I crept out of the bed as stealthily as I could, but how stealthily can you creep away from people you are spooning with? I went outside and found my husband blissfully sleeping away unaware of the night-time drama inside. Insanely jealous and not caring whether I woke him or not, I unzipped his sleeping bag and attempted to crawl in with him. The US Army did not intend for GIs to have company in their sleeping bags. Not able to get in next to him, I discovered my only option: I laid down directly on top of him. Even though the bag would not accommodate more occupants, it could handle more rotund occupants than my 150-pound sweetie. We had not been married so long that such togetherness was actually that unpleasant. I drifted off as the sun rose. Was John able to sleep? If asked, I would have said, "Frankly my dear, I don't give a damn."

25

Sugar in the Wine

June 24, 1970: Paramount releases the movie Catch-22, *based on the novel of the same name by Joseph Heller. In a parody of the military mentality, a World War II bombardier tries desperately to be declared insane so he won't have to fly any more missions.*

June 24, 1970: Congress repeals the Gulf of Tonkin Resolution which started the deployment of combat troops in Vietnam in 1964.

"Abandoned." That's what it says on my great-grandmother's divorce decree. A divorce in our family, neither common nor acceptable in polite society at that time, perplexed me as a child. The only explanation I remember hearing compared the marriage to typical German-French relations: always at war. I never met my great-grandmother, but I knew about her because my mother often spoke of her Grandma Stolzenberger, born Anna Caroline Augusta Bachus, then Marchend, and later Stolzenberger. Grandma emigrated from near Berlin to the United States in 1881 as a 13-year-old girl. Her three-generation immigrant family settled in Wisconsin. Less than two years later, in 1883, she married a French-speaking Belgian immigrant, a Walloon, 16 years her senior, August Michel Joseph Marchend.

August had come from Liège, Belgium, near the German border. According to Liège parish records of births, marriages, and burials, his family had lived in the working-class Outremeuse area of Liège, literally translated as the other side of the Meuse River. The son of a stonemason whose family had lived within a few blocks of each other since the 1600s practicing a variety of trades, including weaving and lacemaking, August somehow became an educated man and worked in America as a clerk and a French teacher. But, as the family story goes, he was a bit of a dreamer and a part-time inventor, somehow managing to travel back and forth to the old country to patent his inventions, while leaving Anna alone with the children, feeling abandoned. Even though he always returned eventually.

They had five children during their ten year marriage, but only three survived childhood. The survivors included my grandmother Rose, the first born, who arrived just a year after the wedding, as well as two younger siblings Eva and Victor. However, Alex, born in 1892, lived only 3 months, and Polly died at age six in 1894, two years after Alex. A year later Anna and August divorced. He never remarried, but at the 1900 Exposition Universelle in Paris, he succeeded in exhibiting one of his inventions, webbed gloves to help shipwreck survivors tread water.

In 1901 Anna, at age 36, traveled with her elderly parents and her three surviving children to Dryver, Kansas, for an arranged marriage to a widowed German immigrant farmer, Wilhelm Stolzenberger, 12 years older than Anna, a man with two grown children. Besides his children and her children, they subsequently had two more of their own, a family of seven. I have been told by relatives that Grandmother Stolzenberger was made of stern stuff, not a lot of warm fuzzies to share with grandchildren, or anyone. But my mother adored her Grandma Stolzenberger.

It was Grandma Stolzenberger who taught Mom to love cooking and baking. She taught her well enough that Mom's first job, summers while in high school, was preparing the noon dinner spread for the town banker's many farmhands. After marriage, cooking became her primary way to show her love: pies for Dad, chocolate pudding for my brother, and *Kuchen* or cakes for me. Everything was homemade, no sparing the sugar, the butter, or the cream. Anything sweet came smothered with hand-whipped whipping cream or topped with ice cream. Ice cream was not an acceptable dessert by itself. It capped whatever she baked. If she served ice cream alone, you knew she was sick.

Each summer in July and August, before air conditioning, we took evening drives in the country with all the car windows rolled down and our hair blowing to escape the heat of the house. Several times a week these trips ended at the open-air farmer's market just outside town. If she had still lived in the country, she would have had her own garden like Grandma Stolzenberger had taught her, but now that she lived in the big city of Bettendorf, one of the Quad Cities straddling the Mississippi River, she had to make do with the farmer's market. Some days she selected huge, deep red tomatoes, still caked with black Iowa mud, so ripe they had started cracking on top, actually bursting. Other days she would choose strawberries or blackberries or raspberries for jam, tasting for the juiciest, a burst of flavor so strong it involuntarily raised her shoulders causing an embarrassed but gleeful smile on her face.

189

The next day she would sterilize canning jars in boiling water while simmering tomatoes or strawberries or boiling corn or green beans in huge pots. All burners on the stove blazed with steaming pots. It didn't matter if the temperature was 100 degrees and the humidity the same. I can picture her hovering over the stove, wooden spoon in hand, wearing her green-checked apron on top of her gray, shirt-waist house dress with the mauve floral splotches. My usually fastidious mother had beads of sweat streaking her face and limp curls, usually combed back, now dangling in her eyes. Her dress developed dark, ever-widening circles under her arms and wet patches down her back. To be sure, she always took a bath promptly at 3:30 Monday through Friday so that she was as freshly attired and coiffured as June Cleaver when my dad walked in the door. On these canning days, I stayed away, seeking a cooler place outside where I could play jacks in the shade.

We had to wait until late summer and early fall when the apples ripened, for the yummiest treat of all, her homemade applesauce laced with cinnamon and generously sweetened with brown sugar. She spent several days of each week peeling apples, coring apples, boiling apples, and using her wooden pestle to push the softened apples through her cone-shaped food press until the sauce oozed through the holes into the over-sized bowl below. Once chilled the result tasted like summer in a bowl. Surely, Mom's applesauce would even have made Grandma Stolzenberger smile.

Several times Mom, tears in her eyes, told me the story of her most cherished childhood memory of her Grandma Stolzenberger. Mom's little sister Edith died of diphtheria at age seven, just before Christmas. The grieving family was quarantined for three weeks, prohibited from even attending Edith's funeral or burial. During that time Grandma would bring them daily care packages. Mom, age 10, waited at the window each day to be the first to spy her Grandma splashing through the sloppy December snow on the dirt road approaching their house. Grandma had to stop just outside the white picket front gate that held the quarantine sign: CARRIER OF DIPHTHERIA: KEEP OUT OF THIS HOUSE. She would try to brush away the snow to make a dry place for her packages. When she had turned and gone, Mom pulled on her galoshes and mushed down the unshoveled front walk quickly retrieving the goodies and carrying them inside to see what Grandma had brought today. This routine continued for the three weeks of the quarantine period including Christmas and into the New Year. Mom's only Christmas present that year was an orange, an exotic treat, left for her by Grandma Stolzenberger on Christmas Day.

Living in Germany I recognized and came to understand a couple of my mother's personality traits, undoubtedly influenced by Grandma Stolzenberger, especially her household efficiency and work-ethic whether tending her flower beds or baking gooey delicacies topped with whipped cream. So it was not a total surprise when Mom and Dad announced they had sprung for tickets to Germany. They were coming to see us, of course, but it felt right that Mom should experience Grandma Stolzenberger's country and its culture. We had heard my parents' voices for three minutes on Christmas Day, but otherwise our only communication consisted of the weekly letters. It was almost a year since we had hugged each other. We were ecstatic!

Having no place in our apartment for Mom and Dad to sleep, I booked them a room at the nearest gasthaus on the main street, three blocks from our apartment. One evening in late June, I met their bus at the Hauptbahnhof, where John had met me almost a year before. It had been a long trip for them with three flights followed by five hours on a bus. After lots of hugs and lots of shoving on luggage to make it fit into the car, I took them directly to the gasthaus, helped them check in and left them with the directions to our apartment for the next morning: two blocks down the main street, jog one block to the right to Arndtstrasse, then first house beyond the corner, number 102. I wrote the address down for them.

The next morning they didn't show up until almost noon. Dad arrived nearly bent in half, puffing and panting from the walk, followed by the climb up our stairs. He had never returned to full strength after his struggle with pancreatitis and months in the hospital my freshman year of high school. I had overestimated his ability to walk. At home it never seemed an issue. He walked from the house to the car and from the car into his office or our church or a grocery store and from there back to the car which took him home to our garage. In Bettendorf, Iowa, he never had to walk farther than across the street, and, due to his father's influence, that suited him fine.

Dad's father, William Veach, called Billy, at age four lost his own father to diseases contracted while serving in the Union Army during the Civil War. Billy's mother left the boy on his uncle's farm for most of his childhood while she went elsewhere to seek her fortune, another husband, or two. Having to earn his own way, with little schooling, Billy learned to drive a mule team and eventually worked for the railroad building bridges. Once Billy could make money, the family reunited, and he supported his twice-widowed, once-divorced mother and a half-sister.

At age 33 Billy, now William, married Myrtle Coen, who taught him his times tables, so he could begin a new career as a builder allowing him to stay closer to home. He always said he never lost money after his first structure, an outhouse. I remember as a child when we visited the county seat of Hutton, Kansas, the pride I absorbed from my father as he pointed out all the important buildings his father William had built: the gigantic 4H sale barn out on the highway, later subdivided into boutique shops, mostly antiques, and the stone high school in town, still serving the area as a community college. Dad, himself a high school student during its construction, talked about loading wheelbarrow after wheelbarrow with rocks, carting them to the stonemasons laying the rock, and unloading them, just to do it all over again every day, all day, all summer vacation in the nearly 100 degree temperatures and matching humidity. He swore he had touched every rock on that building.

William worked his son ruthlessly so Dad would pay attention in school and learn to use his mind, not his body, to make a living. William succeeded; Dad loathed physical exercise and read incessantly. My favorite childhood memory is sitting on the arm of his overstuffed chair listening to him read from my stack of *Little Golden*

Books: The Little Engine that Could, The Poky Little Puppy, and many others. He would stop reading and let me supply the words from memory.

Now as Dad plopped his heaving body into a kitchen chair, I tried to brighten the mood by asking, "Did you have breakfast at the gasthaus?" I knew it was included.

"They gave us some coffee, thank goodness, and some really hard rolls with jam, no cereal or eggs or even toast," Dad said, dismissing the crusty German brotchen that John and I loved as "some really hard rolls."

"Can I give you some cereal?" I offered.

"No, no. What time is it? We'll have lunch soon, won't we?"

"Yes, I can set out some cold-cuts, chips, and fruit any time," I said trying to keep Dad happy, but knowing that I would be serving him the "really hard rolls" to make into a sandwich rather than the doughy, sliced Wonder bread he was used to.

After lunch I noticed Dad twirling a lock of hair, a habit he had when uncomfortable or nervous. "Patty," he asked, not quite looking me in the eye, "did you know our room didn't have its own bathroom? The toilet was down the hall one way and the tub the other direction . . . no shower."

"Yes. That's typical in Germany. Private bathrooms are a luxury. You might find some in a deluxe downtown hotel. They'd be pricey, and you'd be a half hour away from our place without a car."

"Now, everything was very clean. I'm not sure anyone else is staying there, so we didn't meet anyone else in the hall, but . . . ," he trailed off still twirling his hair.

As we talked, his eyes, and Mom's, too, wandered from mine to rest on the teeny stove and refrigerator in the kitchen or on the drooping wallpaper and torn sofa upholstery once we moved into the living room after lunch. I could tell they were trying hard not to show their dismay at our garret apartment.

I was relieved when John and Dad left to pick up our rental car for touring, a VW bus, cheap but spacious with lots of room for luggage. When they returned, John, anxious to give it a spin, insisted we do a local tour. We drove past the Mannheim American High School and Turley Barracks, so Mom and Dad could see where we worked. Besides the MPs Turley was also home to two transportation battalions. Dad's eyes popped at the acres and acres of khaki green army trucks parked just outside Turley, accumulating dust, waiting for a war. There were fields of semi-truck tractors, fields of enclosed semi-trailers, fields of open semi-trailers, and fields of pallet trailers.

"If I could use those for just one day, none of us would ever have to work again," Dad exclaimed.

Our next stop was the *Wasserturm* in downtown Mannheim. John parked so we could walk through the gardens, enjoying the playful fountains and the profuse flowers, changed frequently so they were always in bloom. Mom, now, was in her element, especially enamored with the tall, bright-red, canna lilies she had never seen before in such masses. She insisted on a picture of her in front of them. It was the first of many: Mom in the multi-colored rose garden in the walled city of Rothenburg-ob-der-Tauber; Mom next to the window boxes overflowing with red petunias in Salzburg, Austria; Mom among the 50

195

shades of pink in the formal gardens at Mad King Ludwig's Bavarian Linderhof Palace; and Mom standing on the edge of a cliff, with craggy, snow-covered mountains behind her, clutching a bouquet of edelweiss, in Murren, Switzerland.

The next day, John being off duty, we took to the road for our day trip to Cologne. Dad, of course, sat in the front passenger seat next to John. Men didn't ride in the back seat in the Midwest in the mid-twentieth century: that was for women and children. After all, he was paying for the rental of the bus, so why shouldn't he sit where there was more leg room? And besides, both John and Dad smoked, cigarettes and pipes, both of them. In the front seat, they could lower their windows and clear much of the smoke, blowing their hairdos to smithereens if they wanted. Dad had driven on vacations that had taken our family to all but five of the 48 contiguous states in the US, so all of us expected him to be the navigator.

He tried to follow the AAA road map he had brought from home. Both Germanies together were slightly smaller than Montana, but a smidge bigger than New Mexico. You could easily travel either of those places with a AAA map. But the population of the Germanies was four times the size of California, the most populous state in the US. A denser population meant more roads, and many of them followed winding medieval routes, too numerous and too labyrinthine to show up on such a large scale map. After a year in Germany, we had found that the most reliable way to get from Point A to Point B was to follow the road signs. You had to know the names of major places in the direction you were heading, but the sign system, a product of German engineering, was both efficient and accurate. You had to have faith. And you had to be alert!

"Ken, you need to help me watch for signs pointing to Cologne, *Köln* in German, K O L N with two dots over the O. Sing out when you see anything," John alerted him.

"Cologne is Köln? Why don't they just call it Cologne?" he asked peevishly. With the map unfolded all over the front seat, he buried himself in it trying to find our location and a road to Köln.

Within five minutes, I was yelling, "John, John. I'm pretty sure that sign back there said Köln to the right."

We went quite a ways before John found a place to get off the road in a farm driveway, turn around, and re-enter the road, gravel crunching and tires screeching, as he had to merge quickly into the on-coming traffic. From the other side, we saw an arrow and the word "Köln," as usual with no road number, pointing toward a narrower road. It didn't look like a major highway, but we knew that didn't mean anything. Even if Dad hadn't been buried in the map, he expected a four-way highway junction with road numbers, a square grid, like at home. And he had the added mind-blowing language confusion, Köln, not Cologne. How could there be two names for the same city?

Thank God we came to the autobahn shortly which provided Dad a more familiar cultural experience, road signs and entrance ramps being similar to the Interstate system at home. Yet it had its cultural idiosyncrasies, too. Used to doing the driving himself, he started with the hair twirling again whenever John slowed down and fell in behind slow-moving trucks rather than automatically moving into the left lane to pass. Dad had no clue that a Mercedes or BMW, legally doing 100 miles per hour or more in the passing lane, had the right of way. They were not expected to stop, or even slow down. If your VW bus got caught in the passing lane, a faster vehicle would flash their lights to indicate they were coming through. Then you were expected to move back into the right lane or, if blocked by a truck, evaporate. Therefore, VW buses, not known for their acceleration or speed, didn't dare pass on a curve if they couldn't see what might be coming up from behind.

As we left the autobahn and entered the snarled confusion of roads in Cologne, John asked Dad to watch the signs for the Cathedral. In the midst of city traffic, Dad tried to guide John down one ways going the wrong way because he didn't understand the international Do Not Enter signs, now used in this country, too, but unknown in the US in 1970. Once we found the Cathedral and a parking lot just beyond, Dad announced that he could not walk the distance back to the Cathedral. So we left the parking lot and spent 15 minutes on the tangle of roads trying to get back to the Cathedral. Of course, there were no parking places in front of or next to the Cathedral, so we drove on. Another 15 minutes later, John found his way back to the Cathedral a third time, now desperate enough to dare to pull into a No Parking Zone long enough to let Dad out before proceeding to the parking lot that we had left a half hour earlier.

Once we made it to the Cathedral, we found Dad resting on a low wall outside the Gothic facade of gables, stepped windows, and double spires pointing 500 feet into the sky. He told us to go ahead inside, that he'd be along shortly. John and I, eager to return after our brief and bitterly cold foray to Cologne on New Year's Day, ushered Mom through the entrance. We halted just inside overwhelmed by the grandeur, the sweep of the nave to the stained-glass windows behind the chancel nearly 500 feet beyond and the majesty of the gigantic clustered columns lining the way while pulling the eye upward to the ceiling nearly 150 feet above. After taking a few minutes for Mom's failing eyes to adjust as much as possible to the soft light, I took her arm for safety, and using our *Michelin Green Guide*, the long, narrow, green-colored guidebook favored by European tourists, we made a detailed circuit of the awe-inspiring interior.

Here's the kicker. An hour later we still had not bumped into Dad, so we went outside to look for him. There he was, in the same spot, chatting with some people from Texas. He knew their whole life story. Being the quintessential warm puppy who could not only make friends with anyone, but loved doing so, he had thoroughly enjoyed his visit to the Cologne Cathedral. However, it took me years to admit this. At the time I remember thinking how much easier it would have been if he had stayed in the car.

On the way home, somewhere north of Frankfurt, we stopped for dinner at a gasthaus, half-timbered like a picture from Grimm's fairytales and tucked amid rows and rows of grapevines climbing the surrounding hills. We helped Mom and Dad choose from the German menu: *Wiener Schnitzel*, breaded veal, and *Spaetzle*, an herbed noodle dish.

Dad grew quite impatient when his meal hadn't arrived after fifteen minutes. "How long has it been since we ordered?" he demanded.

"Now, Ken, I'm sure it will be here soon. Let's be patient." Mom soothed.

I explained it could easily be a half an hour or more before our food arrived. Germans, who can't afford to eat out often, plan to spend the evening and get their money's worth. No table is ever used twice in the same evening. Polite food service does not rush the diners, but allows them to savor the experience and enjoy the time with their companions. Actually, the cook begins to prepare the food only after it is ordered.

"If it's going to be a while, maybe we should sample some of that German wine that you ordered," Dad suggested. Mom nodded.

I was horror struck. My Methodist, teetotaling parents wanted to order *Weisswein*?

When the wine arrived, Mom started to take the glass and realized it wasn't chilled like a CocaCola. "Patty, can you ask them to put some ice in mine?" she requested. I thought John was going to crawl under the table just thinking about the sacrilege of diluting deliciously fruity Riesling wine.

Quickly I explained: "Mom, ice is a luxury. You saw our refrigerator . . . it's pretty typical for Germans. If I ask for ice, they prob'ly won't have it or it might not be clean . . . not safe to drink. They use ice like in an ice box for refrigeration." I didn't even get into the common German notion that cold is bad for the stomach.

Another kicker: after the first sip, she involuntarily scrunched her nose from the taste, sour by her standards, and stirred a heaping spoonful of sugar into her glass.

We didn't look forward to next week's trip on the Romantic Road.

26

━━━━◆

Romantic Road Trip

Next week the four of us set off down Germany's Romantic Road to Rothenburg ob der Tauber. A medieval castle, begun in the 10th century, sat above the Tauber River with the sprawling town around it. *Burg* in German means a fortified town. The area received its official charter in the 12th century, and it rapidly expanded in the 13th century with walled fortifications and many buildings which still exist.

Before World War II, Rothenburg, internationally recognized for its medieval architecture, had passed restrictive laws to control any changes to its historic character. Although it had suffered some aerial bombardment from American forces, in the spring of 1945, six soldiers from the US 12th Infantry, 4th Division, were sent across enemy lines to save the city. Holding a white flag, they offered the Germans in Rothenburg a three-hour window for surrender or the town would be bombed to the ground. In spite of an order from Hitler to fight to the end, the German commander gave up the town, thus saving it for posterity. Thank goodness!

We checked into our guesthouse. One look around confirmed that we were smack-dab in the middle of the historic action just across the square from the ornately timbered *Rathaus* or City Hall. On one side we shared a wall with the *Ratstrinkstube* or former tavern next door, where the medieval city fathers often went for further discussion while imbibing in the local wine. Now, every hour on the hour, the tourist hordes gathered in the market place to see and hear the building's *Glockenspiel*. On either side of the central clocks, two windows opened and mechanical figures re-enacted the legend of the *Meistertrunk* from the Thirty Years War in the 17th century. Highly romanticized, the legend goes like this: in 1631 Count Tilly, the Catholic general, offered to spare the Protestant town if anyone could chug a gigantic tankard of local wine, more than three quarts. Supposedly, retired Mayor Nusch did just that! Over three hundred years on, the Thirty Years War feels remote to tourists on holiday, and the Meistertrunk legend paints it as light-hearted. The suffering of the citizens in the carnage of war dims as only a faint whisper in history, yet the reality of what happened involved more blood than wine. Scholars estimate that 50 percent of the population in that region perished due to the battles, atrocities, disease, famine, and disruption of commerce produced by that war, perhaps the worst catastrophe for Germans until the 20th century.

Chuckling about the irony of the term *Rathaus* for the meeting place of the city politicians, Dad took to the cobbled streets on foot, able to go at his own pace, with plentiful benches available for rest. He could return to his room for a nap whenever he wanted. Mom, John, and I walked the mile-long town walls and climbed the Harvest Tower near the western gate, savoring the views of the countryside, not the neat rectangular fields like Iowa, but the higgledy-piggledy misshapen patches along curving medieval paths. Back on the street, we all delighted in the ubiquitous flower baskets in window sills and hanging next to doorways. In the formal gardens, Mom couldn't help stopping to smell the roses at every opportunity. We took a break each afternoon for a treat paid for by Mom, a slice of black forest cake or a rum ball, always with whipped cream, and we dined each night with white wine, always with sugar but without ice for Mom.

From Rothenburg we wound our way along the Romantic Road to picturesque Nuremberg, named for its castle on the *Berg* or hill. We stayed at the Bavarian American Hotel, originally an annex built by the Nazi Party to Nuremberg's Grand Hotel in 1936. At that time, the most modern building in the city, it had guest and service elevators, the main public rooms were air-conditioned, and the hotel had its own water chlorination plant and automatic emergency-lighting system, all controlled from an engineering room, 60 feet below street level. During World War II, Air Marshall Hermann Goering stayed in suite 379 every summer for an annual Nazi Party conference staffed by the Grand Hotel next door. Those two weeks per year were the only time the building was used. It operated as a party house, a perquisite for Nazi Party leaders. After the war the Americans quickly repaired bomb damage to the upper stories so that the hotel could accommodate the judges and attorneys participating in the Nuremberg War Trials that began in November of 1945. By the 1970s the US Armed Forces operated it for their servicemen and families—us!

Sometime in the middle of the night, an alarm jolted me out of a deep sleep. I heard people running in the halls, and the alarm continued at a pitch that threatened to turn an ordinary human into a babbling idiot. Getting out was not an option, but an imperative! John pulled on his jeans and grabbed his jacket from a chair by the door. He threw me my raincoat to cover my nightie, and we joined the chaos in the halls. Over the alarm I heard someone yelling, "Bomb." We pounded on Mom and Dad's door. We waited an eternity as Mom located her trench coat to put over her and then would not leave until she found her purse in the dark. Dad had his bedroom slippers right by the bed, but then after pulling on his trousers, he insisted on fumbling in the dark for his pipe, tobacco, and lighter. We helped them down five flights of stairs in the dark, all of those ultra-modern, 1930's elevators shut down in case of fire.

Once outside we followed the other guests crossing the street toward the Frauentorturm, one of the round towers at a gate in the town wall. A wide stairs led down into the former moat, now a garden. A crowd was forming among the trees at the base of the medieval wall. We waited in the damp cool night air. Yes, we were hopefully at a safe distance and below street level, but what of those searching the hotel? And what would happen if we had nothing but Mom's purse, Dad's pipe, and the clothes, or rather pajamas, on our backs? Dad's jitters were compounded when he found he didn't have enough tobacco left for a pipeful. Thankfully, John discovered that he happened to have a full pouch in his jacket pocket.

After a couple of hours, hotel personnel gave the all-clear informing us that there had, indeed, been a bomb threat, but they had swept the building and found nothing. My imagination went to work overtime. How do you sweep an entire hotel, every nook and cranny, and

205

confidently say, "It was only a threat"? Had they gone through the attic and looked behind every rafter and beam? What about the basement, perhaps still filled with boxes of posters and banners and leaflets from the Nazis? What about the spiders and cockroaches? Did they disturb them or avoid those places? What about the multiple suitcases in every room? Did they look beneath the underwear, the dirty clothes, even the dirty underwear? In spite of our exhaustion, we didn't especially want to go back to our rooms, but what choice did we have in our state of undress—spend the rest of the night in the train station around the corner? So, reluctantly, we marched back in among the disheveled herd of other guests in pajamas and rode the elevators up to our rooms, but we didn't sleep any more that night.

So, even on vacation in Germany, we couldn't escape the Vietnam Conflict. Kent State had produced global shock waves causing a surge in protests overseas just as it had in the US. Although European students weren't being drafted, they had been demonstrating in solidarity with their American peers for several years. There were no draft offices or ROTC departments on campuses for overseas demonstrators to target, but there were US military installations. Bomb threats produced a disruption that proved effective for the non-violent who felt compelled to be disruptive but did not want to actually hurt anyone. No, we didn't agree with hotel bomb threats, and we also didn't appreciate being a target for a cause that would have found us a sympathetic audience. More schizophrenia. We had dodged any mention of the war, hippies, or war protests with Mom and Dad. Our method of conflict resolution was conflict avoidance. After all, we had missed them terribly, loved them deeply, and were spending their three-week vacation in constant togetherness. Who wanted to ruin that? But even through our silence, the war still had given us a poke.

Without much sleep we left the Romantic Road and traveled into Bavaria, visiting Munich and the Hofbräuhaus built in 1589. In the famous beer hall, we ordered our beer *helles,* or light, in *ein Mass,* or a stein, and drank accompanied by the lively oompah band. Capitalizing on the boisterous *Gemütlichkeit*, cordiality and good cheer, in 1920 Hitler and the National Socialist Party had chosen the Hofbräuhaus for their first meeting place. Ironic!

From Munich we drove to Berchtesgaden, Hitler's Bavarian retreat, where he spent more time than he did in his Berlin office. His house, the Berghof, had stood on the Obersalzburg, a high plateau nearly 1500 feet above the town with stunning alpine views all the way to Salzburg, Austria, 19 miles away. The area became a center for Nazi officialdom spread with luxury homes for such henchmen as Air Marshall Goering and Martin Bormann, Hitler's secretary. It included barracks for SS troops and guest houses for visitors, a kindergarten and a gymnasium with athletic fields, a greenhouse and a teahouse. However, perhaps at the time of our visit in 1970, the most spectacular part of the Obersalzburg was never seen by most visitors: the vast underground bunker system equipped with apartments and supply rooms.

In 1952 the Bavarian state destroyed any remnants of the Nazi stronghold lest it become a future shrine for Neo-Nazis. By 1970 natural vegetation covered the past. One of the few buildings left standing was the rambling former Platterhof Hotel, the original 19th century Obersalzburg resort that predated the Nazi Party, now repaired and renovated by the US like the Bavarian American Hotel in Nuremberg, to provide accommodation to American troops and their families for rest and recreation. For an astounding two dollars per room per night, we stayed in the renamed General Walker Hotel. The rates escalated with rank, the only time it was good to be a grunt, not a king or a general. Our view stretched across Bavaria and through a northern pass to Salzburg. Toward the southwest loomed a ridge of peaks among the highest in Germany ending behind us with the towering height of the Hoher Goell. Down a ridge from its summit perched the Kehlstein at over 6,000 feet altitude, the mountaintop site of Hitler's Kehlsteinhaus, referred to by English-speakers as Hitler's "Eagle's Nest" or sometimes his "Teahouse."

From near the General Walker Hotel on the Obersalzburg, buses departed regularly to the Kehlsteinhaus entrance, more than 2000 feet above. The narrow road made two-way traffic impossible, allowing only one bus to travel the road at a time. Our bus wound its way nearly four miles through tunnels and along hairpin curves gaining altitude with every turn of the wheels. Upon reaching the top, it deposited us next to a solid wall of granite. After a short walk, we entered a dark, damp tunnel bored into the mountainside leading to an elevator. When the doors opened, our eyeballs reverberated from the sight of its polished brass interior.

A discrete sign read Otis. It was an American elevator! It lifted us over 400 feet straight up through the rock to the top of the cliff. One step outside confirmed that the place deserved to be known as the Eagle's Nest. Walking around was a dizzying proposition for those without wings, so we had tea and tried to keep our feet firmly planted on the rock beneath us. Hitler only used this massively expensive eyrie, a 50th birthday present, a few times.

The **Treaty of Versailles** [ending World War I] . . . seemed to have opened an era where financial transactions ruined commercial prudance [sic]. Enormous debts ruined the German people financially and morally without leaving any chance of commercial recovery. The former kingdom had been split apart . . . . During this great depression Hitler appeared and encouraged the German population with his enthusiasm and confidence in a new and better Germany. . . . we have attempted to publish a completely neutral documentation about **Adolf Hitler's** exceptional ascension to the "**Führer**" of the German Nation. We also try to explain why millions of people were inclined to favour Adolf Hitler's "Regime." The war was not only hatred and racial discrimination, but also patriotical [sic] love and defense. One should perhaps try not to confuse those different ideas.
—*Obersalzburg: The Biography of the III. [sic] Reich,*a German tourist booklet 1970

John Explores Hitler's Eagle's Nest

Some would say Hitler must have been mad to unleash the destruction of World War II and the Holocaust upon the world, but in Bavaria, in the nineteenth century, they had a king commonly referred to as Mad King Ludwig, so mad that he emptied the state coffers building many residences. So, what's so mad about that? Isn't that what most kings did? In 1864 Ludwig II of Bavaria came to the throne unexpectedly at age 18. By age 25 he had supported the losing side in the Austro-Prussian War and lost Bavaria to Prussia in the resulting German Unification. He had lost most of his power, except in local matters, and became a pawn of Prussia. He consoled himself and sought to bolster his historic legitimacy by immersing himself in a romanticized version of the past. Literally, he escaped the reality of his current political situation by losing himself in a world of fantasy using all of his personal, family, and state resources to fund fanciful architectural projects.

In Mad King Ludwig's Bavaria, our first stop was at Lake Chiemsee where we boarded a ferry to Herrenchiemsee Palace, in the middle of Germany's largest lake. Here, in 1878, Ludwig bought an island on which to build, not just a palace inspired by Louis XIV's Versailles, but a replica of it. Almost every country in Europe has its version of Versailles, every monarch feeling compelled to keep up with Louis XIV, who set the standard for extravagance. Unfortunately, his descendant Louis XVI and wife Marie-Antoinette eventually paid the political price at the guillotine. Only some days it's good to be the king!

We entered by the Grand Staircase marveling at the Classical marble sculptures surrounding us, guarding their niches. In the Hall of Mirrors with 17 arches just as in Versailles, we mugged and watched our antics reverberate infinitely into mirror upon mirror down the length of the hall. In the State Bedchamber, although Ludwig never slept there, dying before the building was completed, he departed from the replica to make his bedroom even bigger than Louis's, resplendent with crystal chandeliers and French rococo gilding. Louis would also have envied Ludwig's indoor toilets, running water, and central heating.

Finally, in the Dining Room, where we expected a lengthy table of many place settings for dinners of state, Mad King Ludwig revealed his true character. Here stood his regal Magic Table, opulently covered in cloth of red and gold to match his Louis XIV ornately carved and gilded chair with red velvet upholstery. The Magic Table, whose name came from a Grimm's fairytale, could be elevated and lowered through a trap door. Its purpose: the reclusive Ludwig could eat alone without even servants to disturb his solitude.

Our heads spinning from the opulence of Herrenchiemsee, we wound our way into the rugged foothills of the Bavarian Alps to Neuschwanstein, probably Ludwig's most famous residence because Walt Disney used it as the inspiration for Sleeping Beauty's castle in Disneyland. Started in 1869, that's after our Civil War, on a spot visible from Hohenswangau Castle where Ludwig grew up, it allowed him to immerse himself in the mythical origins of his country as depicted in the operas of Richard Wagner. By that time, castles were an anachronism, feudal warfare having disappeared centuries earlier. Only Mad King Ludwig was still building castles.

While Herrenchiemsee embodied the Baroque ideals of Absolutism, in Neuschwanstein Ludwig sought the chivalric ideals of the Christian kings during the Middle Ages as glorified in music by Wagner. The murals in the Salon and Singers Hall commemorated the heroes of *Parsifal* and *Lohengrin* portraying the German version of the Holy Grail legend. Lohengrin travels in a boat drawn by a swan, hence the name given to the castle *Neuschwanstein* or New Swan Stone. Although still under construction, Ludwig actually did live here upon the completion of the interior of his private rooms for all of 172 days before his death.

So, was the Mad King, indeed, mad? And how did poor Ludwig die? He had obsessed over his building projects, eventually defaulting on incredible debt, and he had ignored the affairs of state. He was rumored to be homosexual, not hopeful for producing an heir. Since the only constitutional way to remove a Bavarian monarch was to have him declared mentally incompetent, desperate family members convened a group of psychiatrists, none of whom ever examined Ludwig, but they declared him insane. He was taken under duress from Neuschwanstein and incarcerated at Castle Berg on Starnberger Lake. He and the head psychiatrist, Dr. Gudden, were both found dead in shallow water three days later.

Actually, it was more like a coup. What we know: Dr. Gudden's body reportedly showed signs of a struggle. Declared drowned, Ludwig, a strong swimmer, had no water in his lungs. Was Ludwig's death accidental, suicidal, or murder? Who was responsible? Unlike the assassination of the Archduke Franz Ferdinand of Austria which triggered World War I, nobody cared enough about pitiful Ludwig to start a war! Poor Ludwig!

From Ludwig's Bavaria in the south of Germany, we crossed the Swiss border enjoying the pastoral, flower-dotted meadows tucked among the spine-tingling peaks of neutral Switzerland where it had been almost 500 years since the last military battle. Hallelujah!

27

Give Peace a Chance

August 24, 1970: Sterling Hall at the University of Wisconsin-Madison is bombed. A truckload of explosives aimed at the Army Math Research Center accidentally hits the physics laboratory killing a researcher and seriously injuring another.

August 29, 1970: Hispanics participate in the Chicano Moratorium in East Los Angeles, their largest antiwar demonstration with 30,000 protesters. Police kill a TV news director and an LA Times reporter.

September 27–30, 1970: President Nixon makes an official visit to Italian President Saragat in Rome, Pope Paul VI in Vatican City, and NATO Southern Command Headquarters in Naples.

After frolicking in the meadows of the Black Forest with flowers in my hair, I didn't attend the peace march in Mannheim that August, but John did. He was one of the clean-shaven guys with short hair dressed in green fatigues, spit-shined black boots, and MP helmets with .45s on their hips. All personnel at the 537th MP Company had been called in for duty. The scale of preparations for this demonstration, unlike previous ones handled by GIs already on duty, indicated larger crowds or larger stakes or both. It was the summer of Kent State, large and menacing was the norm now.

Not wanting our car with US military plates to be parked anywhere near an anti-US military demonstration, I drove him to work, through the main gate on Grenadier Strasse whose electronic chain link barriers stood wide open. We passed under the white banner overhead reading "Turley Barracks" and then proceeded along the grassy parade ground to the 537th MP Company in the back corner. All the red stone buildings pre-existed World War I. Turley originally had been the Kaiser Wilhelm Kaserne. Now it belonged to the US Army wrested from the Germans who had used it through two world wars. Everything seemed quiet and as usual except the white wooden sawhorse that rested near the gate waiting to be pulled into place out front, a boundary before the gate, not to be crossed, establishing a definite, but feeble perimeter. I kissed John good-bye and headed home. The gray VW Bug, at least, was safely in Feudenheim with me, but John was not.

My husband was policing a demonstration. He would be there to protect US Army property, Turley Barracks. Why couldn't the world just give peace a chance, like John Lennon's song? My mind worried the situation like an insistent tongue trying to dislodge a raspberry seed from between two molars. I couldn't dislodge that tune either.

I hummed, "All I am saying is give peace a chance."

Neither John nor I harbored any gung-ho resentment for hippies, often students, like the hawks did. In fact, we wondered if things were different, would we be the protestors? On the other hand, unlike riot police today in their body armor, John wore no protective gear beyond his helmet, a helmet that resides today in our toy box for the grandchildren, a helmet light enough that children can play dress up in it. What if the crowd turned ugly and the students started attacking the police? How could he defend himself? There would be many, many more students than there were MPs.

"All I am saying is give peace a chance," floated through my head.

Also, horrible to contemplate: history is peppered with incidents where a crowd became unruly and panicky troops over-reacted, for example the Boston Massacre or Bloody Sunday in St. Petersburg. Kent State was not the only example, just the most recent. Would the peace demonstration be, indeed, peaceful?

Here it came again: "Give peace a chance."

I tried to settle my nerves by eating. Chocolate usually helped anything, but after one bite, I put down the dark-coated marzipan bar, my stomach too tied in knots to welcome food. I tried to write a letter home, but I couldn't write about my fear. Our parents didn't need me to add worry to their loneliness. Anything from ordinary, everyday life sounded too banal. Who could care that we went to the PX yesterday, or had bratwurst for lunch? What did it matter? I wrote, and crumpled up the sheet of paper, and wrote, and crumpled, wrote, crumpled.

I still couldn't quit humming: "All I am saying is give peace a chance."

Next, I tried to read, wanting to lose myself in a character's troubles. Unfortunately, my current read was Kurt Vonnegut's most recent novel *Slaughterhouse Five*. John and I had been reading our way through the works of Vonnegut, who had been in the Writer's Workshop at Iowa during my years as an English major. As a lowly undergrad, I never had a class from him, but he was a

216

legend on campus. In *Slaughterhouse Five* the main character, Billy Pilgrim, is a US soldier, a POW being held in Dresden, where he survives the Allied firebombing that levels Dresden during World War II. In my imagination Billy looked much like John in his fatigues. Not a helpful distraction.

"All I am saying is give peace a chance."

Having no telephone or television, I had no idea what might be happening beyond my apartment. How many protestors turned out? What was their mood? Did they march to Turley Barracks? Did they keep going or did they try to force entry? It was late, well after dark, when Frau Schaeffer's telephone rang, late enough that I hoped it wouldn't be for her, but I had to wait until she shuffled through her bedroom door, down the stairs, and into her study to answer.

Sure enough, she called up to me, "Frau P-o-w-o-o-o-l, telephone."

I scrambled down the stairs. It had to be John, the MPs would have our address, but not Frau Schaeffer's telephone number.

"Hi, Hon. It's me," he said, "it's over."

"And everything's okay . . . no problems?"

"Everything's okay," he sighed. "They lined us up, turned us toward the street, and spaced us, arms outstretched, fingertip to fingertip, circling Turley. We were so fierce-looking in our green cotton fatigues, those students took one look and ran all the way down Friederich Ebert Strasse" he chuckled. "Seriously, I guess this was mostly about payday. It's tomorrow, and the scuttlebutt says there's over a million dollars cash in the headquarters safe. Wanna' pick me up? I'm beat, headed straight to bed, but I wouldn't mind some company."

The Armed Forces theaters had refused to show *Easy Rider*, the counter-culture hit film. After experiencing the hysteria of *M*A*S*H*, it was not hard to understand. *Easy Rider*, an international sensation, had won the award at Cannes for Best First Work and had two Oscar nominations. Made for under a million dollars, it earned over 60 million worldwide within the first few years. By summer it was still playing in a downtown Mannheim theater. We knew we could see it there, but we didn't want to spend what to us was a huge sum of money to watch it in German. Word got around that some showings were not dubbed, the dialogue in the original English with German subtitles. So next time we were downtown, we checked it out and found that a subtitled showing was beginning soon. We splurged on the admission.

Our friend Steve, being a photography major, had talked about the film incessantly, especially the hand-held camera sequences and the natural out-door lighting as God had intended, both ground-breaking and a significant departure from the classic Hollywood tradition. The music, too, was revolutionary. Rather than an original musical score, the film incorporated "found" music, songs previously recorded by such icons as Bob Dylan, The Byrds, The Band, Jimi Hendrix, and others. For sure, this movie departed from traditional youth films; it was no *Pillow Talk* or *Gidget* or *Beach Blanket Bingo!*

The subject matter was as ground-breaking as the cinematography and music. The tagline on the posters read, "A man went searching for America. And couldn't find it anywhere . . ." What we couldn't find was a way to identify with characters who made a small fortune smuggling cocaine into the US from Mexico, and we were too naive to realize they were smoking dope around the campfire, as history would reveal, real marijuana on the set. The mostly-stoned stars Peter Fonda, Dennis Hopper, and Jack Nicholson ad-libbed the lines. No script actually existed; it went into production with a list of protagonists and an outline. The plot pitted the long-haired bikers, Wyatt, named for Wyatt Earp, and Billy, for Billy the Kid, against the southern backwoods rednecks.

But again, our schizophrenia. The cocaine-dealing aside, we did anguish at the division revealed in our country, the counterculture, sometimes referred to as the youth culture, versus the silent majority, as President Nixon called them, those who believed in the nation's leaders. Parents couldn't understand their own young people. The older generation had made sacrifices in defeating Hitler and Japan and saving the world for posterity from the Holocaust and Fascism. Now those parents couldn't understand why their children, their posterity, were not stepping up to the plate to follow their parents' example? And those children couldn't understand the tradition-bound, narrow viewpoint of their parents, those who followed the current leaders like sheep, like the Germans had followed Hitler. Vietnam was not World War II. While the US Civil War often pitted brother against brother in battle, emotionally the Vietnam-era culture pitted parents against their kids.

While the kids protested and the elders made political speeches, American soldier boys, like Wyatt and Billy in *Easy Rider's* shocking conclusion, were dying.

September brought the new school year and major disappointment. The previous year teachers could request their subs, and I had worked every day requested, no days off to play bridge like the officers' wives, so I had racked up more sub days than anyone else. This year some muckety-muck, high-ranking officer's wife had objected because she didn't get many days of work last year. Of course, her husband applied pressure, and the school had a new substitute policy. To make sure everyone on the sub list had a "fair" opportunity to work—and knew when they could play bridge—they cut the list in half and rotated the two halves every other month. I was out of work for September, my last name *Paul* landing me on the second half of the list. I could work in October, but then not in November. December, with the winter holidays, consisted of only two school weeks. I would not be called in January. One and a half months of work possible during the entire first semester!

Since I couldn't work, we took off traveling again, this time to the Matterhorn near Zermatt, Switzerland, accessible only by train, then over Simplon Pass literally dropping into Italy. Immediately, we realized the difference in culture. Unlike the formal, well-organized Germans, perhaps boisterous in the beer halls, but quiet and reserved on the streets, the lively Italian street scene amused us. Through our hotel window, we enjoyed watching the exuberance as men called loudly to friends, "Eh, Giovanni" or "Eh, Guiseppe," and jay-walked through traffic to greet each other with arms outstretched, men embracing men, enthusiastically clapping each other on the back. Women greeted each other with a kiss on each cheek and usually found something hilarious to share with their friend, causing both to throw their heads back in raucous laughter. Although these people greeted each other as if they hadn't been together in years, we suspected they actually lived in close proximity in the neighborhood and probably hadn't seen each other that day.

And the Italian food amazed us. The inexpensive family restauranteurs with their checkered tablecloths and cheap, plentiful chianti provided fabulous food at prices we could afford. Pastas and sauces like we had never eaten in Iowa! And they treated us like long-lost relatives. When we weren't eating, we reveled in the paintings of Botticelli, Titian, and Raphael and the architectural ingenuity of Bernini, Michelangelo, and Brunelleschi. We delighted in the broad, monumental piazzas and the narrow, winding, medieval passages as we traveled south through Venice, Florence, and Rome.

But in Rome we weren't the only Americans in town. President Nixon had also picked late September as the perfect time for a visit, so every protest-minded Italian flooded into the city. Our pension proprietor politely recommended that we not park our car with an American Forces license plate, our poor old, scummy, gray Bug, not exactly an emblem of American affluence, on the public streets. Mobs were looting and burning throughout the city, attacking anything connected with the US, especially cars. They strongly recommended a secure parking garage several blocks away. It cost more than our room. So, we moved on to Naples. So did Nixon. Once again, we had the added burden of secure parking. Suddenly, the quaint family restaurants became unaffordable for us! We kept counting our lire, our Swiss francs, and our dollars. Did we have enough for the gas to get home? Another poke from the war.

28

Enough!

"Frau, P-o-w-o-o-o-l," Frau Schaeffer called to me as I entered the house one day in early October. She popped her head out the kitchen door to ask, "Are you working this year at the school? Will you need the telephone?"

"Yes," I replied. "I hope so."

She looked at her feet as she said in a soft voice, "I didn't know. No calls have come."

How could I explain to her about the new system? I didn't know myself how things would work out. The turnover of teachers at US dependent schools overseas was much like the turnover of military forces; the commitment was only for a couple of years. By then, many young teachers had had their overseas adventure or found a husband, often going home or sometimes moving to a different part of the world. So, I knew I would have to build my credibility with the staff again, not quite from scratch, but I could not expect to pick up where I left off the previous spring.

With Frau Schaeffer I dodged the real issue and chose a simpler reply, "It's still early in the year. Teachers don't need subs early in the year."

She shrugged as she usually did at some point in every conversation and went back in to tend the steaming pot on her stove, her usual cabbage concoction, the odor overwhelming me as I trudged up the stairs. I narrowly slipped through my own door uselessly hoping the vinegar and cabbage smell wouldn't follow.

What was the point, I wondered? By the time I established myself with new staff, I would leave. John's two years would be finished in February. I grabbed my latest novel and plopped into my reading chair. Who would have thought that all the time in the world to read could become boring? I longed for my own classroom, my own lesson plans, my own students. I longed for my own aha moments with them. I even longed to own those times when a lesson didn't work, when I needed to be the biggest learner in the room, not just the poor slob who happened to be subbing and reaped the misery of another teacher's poor planning or inadequate classroom management. I longed to fill my days with the work for which I had prepared. I longed to go home.

That afternoon John arrived home from work with a silly grin, obviously pleased with himself, his face said, "Ask me, come on, ask me?" So, I did.

"What's got your motor racing?"

"Well, today I was alone in the office with nothing to do, so I entertained myself looking through the personnel files. Guess who has the highest score in the company on the AFQT?" That was the army test similar to the IQ.

"I would guess the Captain, but if that were true, we probably wouldn't be playing this game, would we?"

"You're right. It's not the Captain. Guess again!"

"Stanley. He's always bragging about how he graduated with honors, always talking about what an important job he's going to have in hospital administration when he gets out."

"Naw, you're guesses aren't close, but you are. You're verrrry close," he said pulling me against him for a kiss.

"You! You're the smartest guy in the company? Nah, that can't be."

"Yep. It's not even close. Now I totally understand why everything is so messed up, why SNAFUs are standard. I thought they were smart. Imagine me in charge?" He pulled a salute, puffed out his chest and stretched as tall as he could on tip-toes. Slowly deflating, he admitted, "Whadda' mess that would be! But regardless it certainly doesn't help me tolerate the BS that runs downhill from all those schmucks!" John vowed to make sure he would never again be anybody's flunkie, scrubbing floors or cleaning latrines.

"Frau P-o-w-o-o-o-l, Frau P-o-w-o-o-o-l," Frau Schaeffer called the next day as she ascended the stairs to our apartment, something she seldom did. "Empty bedroom furniture. Everything. A man brings new today."

New bedroom furniture? What was happening? We loved our antique, hand-carved, mahogany bedroom furniture. It made us feel like a king and queen, except, of course, for the tilting mattress section at the foot of each bed that didn't fit the bed frame. Maybe we were getting new mattresses? That would be worth a hassle. In that case, less ornate might be okay.

I cleared everything out of the wardrobes and dresser and piled it high all over the living room, kitchen table, and even across the sides of the tub. In the afternoon a delivery man showed up with our new bedroom furniture. It was made of plywood and obviously only new to us. My heart sank, but I waited to see the mattress. After everything was set up, he asked me a question in German. I could only shrug like Frau Schaeffer and shake my head. I had no idea what he wanted. He began looking around the apartment, under the piles of clothing, until he found the six mattress sections. He smiled and placed them in the bed frame, puzzled when two of them didn't fit. He punched them in as far as they would go. Then he, too, shrugged and left.

Soon I heard Frau Schaeffer on the stairs again. "You like new furniture? My daughter tells me you not like old furniture, so I get new."

I was flabbergasted. We didn't like our beautiful old furniture straight out of a castle? She traded it for this plywood stuff, thinking we would like it better? Then I remembered running into her daughter in the Commissary, the daughter married to a US army officer. She had been most solicitous of how we liked the apartment. Did everything work? She worried that her aging mother was not able to stay on top of things any longer. She was frankly glad someone else was in the house with her *Mutter*. I had told her about the mattress sections not fitting the bed frame, thinking perhaps she might have her mother replace the two sections, a small thing that would greatly add to our comfort. Oh, my!

Addressing Frau Schaeffer while trying not to show my deep disappointment, frankly trying not to cry, I gulped, "It's fine. Fine."

She started down the stairs, but turned back to add, "It was very expensive, very expensive. The man . . ." she hushed her voice and whispered, "is Jewish, you know."

Too stunned to speak, I watched her back as she shut her bedroom door behind her. Thank God, she was gone! That whisper killed any pity I had felt for her, the poor mother alone with four children.

Only a few days later, John came rushing up the stairs, out of breath, waving mail in the air. He had received his results from the LSAT test, the entrance test for law school. A few months earlier he had spent a long Saturday morning in Heidelberg taking the exam. He hadn't been in school for over a year and a half, and he hadn't had access to any preparation materials, let alone a preparation class. He had simply filled out the form, attached a check, and showed up on the scheduled day to take the exam.

Here were his results. He had lacked the nerve to open them, so we both took a deep breath as he tore away the envelope. A quick comparison of his score and the scores required by the University of Iowa and law schools in nearby states showed that he needed to start filling out applications. We weren't completely jubilant as Iowa would be his stretch application, but several other nearby state universities should be a comfortable Plan B. We never considered leaving the Midwest. We needed to be near family, as close as we could get.

The next day, just before noon, I was the one who arrived home, my arms full of wurst, apples, and brotchen purchased in the shops on the Main Street. When I opened the front door, I found the hall and stairwell choked with smoke. Hand over my nose and mouth in an attempt to filter the air, I could see Frau Schaeffer's stove through her open kitchen door. She never left any of her doors open. Flames shot several feet high above a skillet. Where was she? Now I was the one yelling up the stairs, "Frau Schaeffer, Frau Schaeffer." Soon, her bedroom door opened and she appeared on the landing, tugging at her robe crazily askew over her nightie. She started coughing in the smoke. By then I was screaming, "Fire." She hurried down the stairs and then could see the flames in the kitchen. I'm not sure exactly what she did to extinguish the blaze, but she did and then emerged from the kitchen, still coughing, motioning for me to open the front door to let in air. Her hands shook. Her breath wreaked of alcohol. She gave me no explanation, just turned back upstairs, and disappeared into her bedroom. What if I hadn't come in when I did?

29

◆——————◆

Father Forgive

"I got it! I got it!" John yelled early in November bounding up the stairs two at a time. "It" was an early release from the army to return to grad school. "We're celebrating New Year's in I-o-wa!" he yelled using three syllables. "No more army BS. No more cleaning latrines or painting the same damn hallway for the tenth time. Profs can be jerks, but they won't surprise me with a transfer to Nam."

"What about law school?" I asked "It doesn't start 'til fall."

"If I stayed here my full hitch, I'd still have to wait six months 'til law school starts. What kind of job could I get for six months, flipping burgers? I might as well draw that GI Bill I earned. We earned. And if I get into Iowa, those hours count as electives anyway."

"That means I can apply for teaching jobs second semester. Yippee . . . no more subbing!" I squealed catching his excitement. "We're outta' here!"

"Just gotta' hold on for two more months. We're gone, between Christmas and New Year's I figure! We're short timers, short timers, shooooort timers," he sang dancing me around the apartment, in and out of doors, around the kitchen table. The Elephant slunk out of the room. He

229

wasn't gone, but he was unhappy. He might have to move in with somebody else.

This news left us with one piece of unfinished business in Germany, visiting Berlin, then divided into East and West Berlin. The German pre-war capital city lay trapped behind the Iron Curtain stranded in the heart of the communist Russian-controlled sector of Germany, the German Democratic Republic or East Germany.

During the Cold War, West Berlin, formerly the French, British and US sectors, became the symbol of democracy. In 1948 the GDR blockaded highway and railroad transportation into West Berlin from the rest of the world intending to starve the free sectors of the city until they were forced to join the Eastern communist block. From June 24th, 1948, until May 12th, 1949, the heroic Berlin Airlift, a combined effort of the British and Americans, flew food, clothing, and medicine into the city and saved West Berlin. Twelve years later by 1961, the millions of defections of Easterners into West Berlin prompted the GDR to erect, virtually overnight, an 86-mile wall separating West and East Berlin. No residents, East or West Berliners, could pass freely between the sectors of the city. It cut off many Easterners from their jobs and from extended families living in the West. It cut off shopping for food, plentiful in the West, but scarce in the East. It imprisoned East Berliners in communist territory.

On my student tour in 1967, I had come to Berlin and passed through Checkpoint Charlie, the American gate in the Wall, into East Berlin. Yes, Americans could go through, but not Germans. I had seen with my own eyes why we didn't want our democracy to fall to Communism. John had not seen it. He needed to know, deserved to know, that the two-year interruption in his education had served some worthwhile purpose. However, I may have felt about meddling in a civil war in Vietnam, I felt defending NATO during the Cold War, even such a small contribution as ours, did matter. To me John's experience in Germany would be incomplete without going to East Berlin.

But could we get there, especially could he get there? For months I had pestered John to find out how a US soldier and his dependent wife, not an American tourist like I had been, could travel through communist East Germany into Berlin. There was a duty train, but how did one get tickets? There was an autobahn, but could anybody drive on it? Surely, there was a border crossing? Who did they let through and what documents were required? What about restaurants or restrooms? Was gas available?

Introducing himself as "Spec 4 Paul," John's inquiries always had resulted in a runaround. So now that we had a definite deadline, I borrowed Frau Schaeffer's telephone and started making calls. Introducing myself as "Mrs. Paul" and using my poshest voice and vocabulary, no one knew whether my husband was a private or a general, but I didn't sound like anybody's preconceived notion of a Spec 4's wife. After a few courteous transfers, I, indeed, reached someone helpful who explained that once in West Berlin, John could sign up for an army-sponsored tour of the Eastern sector. He would need to wear his Class A uniform and his insignia would have to match exactly that on his service ID issued back at the Jasper County Court House in Newton, Iowa, the day he reported for induction. In other words, he would have to appear to be a buck private. If any detail was amiss, the GDR would consider him a spy. Further, I would not be able to accompany him unless I got a new duplicate passport without the stamp in the back declaring that I was a US Army Dependent. That would take money and three months. We had neither, so John would have to go into the East without me. That was fine; after all I had been there three years before. This trip was John's turn.

But how could we, especially he, get to Berlin? I found out the duty train required making arrangements many weeks, even months, in advance. No time for that. You could drive on one particular autobahn, no exiting for food or gas, passing through East German checkpoints on your own, with all the same stipulations about being regarded as a spy. It sounded like a John Le Carré espionage novel, too chilling. What if our 17-year-old Bug picked that time and place for a break down? But we had one more option, last resort, we could fly on a commercial aircraft, as I had done three years prior. But could we possibly afford the tickets?

The next day I withdrew all of our savings account except the amount we had agreed to keep aside for a basic used car, one with wheels, when we got home. Then, I went to the air charter office for American dependents and booked, at our expense, my flight home from Frankfurt Rhein-Main to JFK with an additional connection to Moline, Illinois. It cost less than Icelandic, and I hoped it would be less eventful.

I didn't know if I had enough money left for tickets to Berlin. Immediately, I headed for the Pan Am office to find out. Indeed, I booked air tickets to Berlin during John's Thanksgiving leave with just enough money remaining to hopefully cover our meals and hotels once we got there. So, when John came up the stairs that afternoon, I had the huge grin. I blurted, "I'm outta' here . . . in 30 days . . . but who's counting? And we're flying to Berlin the week before!" I caught a breath before admitting, "Of course, we're broke . . . flat broke . . . but hopefully I'll have a job lined up, a real job, by the time you get home at the end of the month. Hopefully! I have to!"

Thus, began our blizzard of applications: John applying to law schools while I filled out teaching applications. Papers were strewn across every horizontal surface in our apartment. We even ate meals standing up.

On Thanksgiving, not a holiday in Germany, in the dark of early morning, we trundled down our stairs with luggage in tow headed for the airport in Frankfurt, on our way to Berlin. Since we hadn't opened our German shutters before we left, quite a surprise greeted us at the front door.

"Oh, my gosh," I exclaimed. "I can't believe this. Where's our car? I can't even see the car!"

"How can I drive through this stuff? How can we possibly get to Frankfurt?" John demanded.

"We'll lose our money if we don't show for the flight," I reminded him.

"I guess we have to try. Maybe, it won't be so foggy when we get out of the neighborhood," he responded, trying to convince himself as much as me.

It did improve as we felt our way north and made progress away from the Neckar and Rhine Rivers; however, approaching the airport in Frankfurt, we came near the Main River and back into impenetrable fog, the worst yet. But we made it and parking was easy. Surprise, the airport was nearly empty. Too stupid to realize this was unusual, we approached the arrivals-departure board: "Canceled, canceled, canceled!" British European Airways had the only flight still departing. It was to Berlin. At the Pan Am counter, they re-ticketed us into the last two seats on the BEA flight. We were ecstatic, until we got into the air.

Frowning, John asked, "How can they see other airplanes?" He had never liked flying.

"There are no other airplanes, silly!" I reminded him. "Everyone else is on the ground."

"Where they belong," he muttered grabbing my hand and squeezing hard.

When we felt the landing gear come down, there was still nothing to be seen out the window but dirty-gray marshmallow fluff. The runway and airport appeared only as we touched down. But we had made it to West Berlin.

After checking into our hotel, we stepped out onto a side street and walked a half block before turning onto the Kurfürstendamm or "Ku-damm," the Champs Élysées of West Berlin, two miles of boutique shops, art galleries, cafes, restaurants, automobile showrooms, nightclubs and luxury hotels. A strange mix of building styles lined the Ku-damm. Originally opened by Bismarck in 1871 as a prestigious thoroughfare leading to his hunting lodge in suburban Grünewald, the architecture generally consisted of Neo-Renaissance stone mansions, grand symmetrical buildings with balustraded balconies and rectangular windows framed by columns and topped by triangular entablatures.

"Look, look up there, John," I exclaimed pointing to the stone above the display windows of one of the luxury store fronts. "See that line of holes. How could that have happened except by a machine-gun?"

"Wow! I think it must be. Look over there," he pointed at the next building, again above street level, where one of the decorative window columns had an upper section and a lower section, missing its middle, evidently blown away. The next building, a modern glass-walled structure, forced us to realize that it must have replaced a 19th-century stone edifice, undoubtedly bombed beyond redemption. From the street level, if you didn't look up, you would never guess.

Traffic filled the roadway, actually a boulevard with two roadways, both lined with trees and separated by a tree-lined median. Down the street in buildings new and old, plate-glass display windows lured shoppers with smart fashions, jewelry, and luxury autos. People, most of them carrying their usual leather briefcases or in GI slang schnitzel bags bulging with purchases, bustled along the sidewalks even though it wasn't yet rush hour. In 1970 it was all about capitalism. Prosperity flourished. The Marshall Plan had worked. This was a happening scene, the ultimate in urban sophistication, allowed by the free movement of people and goods in a democratic society.

We quickly fell into the pedestrian flow heading for the subway in hopes of getting to the viewing platform before dark to look across the Wall into Potsdamer Platz. The subway line, like the city itself, was cut by the Wall, so after emerging from the underground, we still faced a considerable walk into what had been the heart of the pre-war city. As we neared our destination, we found ourselves on deserted streets among bombed out buildings, just shells. At street level on one side of the street, we saw former shops with doors and windows boarded up or bricked closed. Any upper stories, when still standing, apartments where German families had lived, still had broken windows, just as the bombs had shattered them. Pigeons flew in and out and their detritus of feathers and droppings littered any flat surfaces, no matter how narrow. These decaying building fronts stood lining the street side-by-side making a wall. Then the buildings stopped and a proper concrete-block wall continued with a tubular concrete top that would make it more slippery for anyone attempting to climb over it. This wall appeared to cross an immense open space, looming above us, blocking any view of what lay behind.

Shortly, just in front of the concrete wall, a billboard appeared. "A strange place for a billboard," I thought. Then I realized it displayed a black and white picture of Potsdamer Platz in 1929, the busiest intersection in the city, even then with luxury automobiles, double-decker buses, a streetcar, and a policeman directing traffic. Monumental buildings provided the backdrop. Just beyond the billboard stood a metal framework of stairs climbing to a platform level, separated from the wall by perhaps 30 feet, but level with the top of the wall. We held the picture in our minds as we climbed.

The stark desolation of the Platz spread before us. Guard towers stood in the distance overlooking a no man's land with a clear view and a clear shot in case any Easterners tried to defect. The open expanse was broken only by beds of large nails and giant X's lined up in double rows following the Wall as far as we could see, as if some giant had been playing a game of jacks, got bored, and placed them in rows outlining the Wall. Our *Michelin Green Guide* explained that they were anti-tank emplacements called Czech hedgehogs. As the sun faded and dusk began to spread, the lights came on, stark and white, so cold, banishing any shadows and exposing every inch to their harsh intensity.

We returned to the sidewalk and continued following the Wall along Ebertstrasse. We passed an abandoned subway entrance, stairs into the ground, now leading nowhere, just to a brick wall. Occasionally, we passed white crosses or floral memorials, each marking where someone had died trying to escape across the wall to the West.

As the sky darkened, we reached the Brandenburg Gate, also starkly lit, the triumphal neoclassical entrance to the city built by Prussian King Frederick Wilhelm II between 1788 and 1791. The Wall ran behind the monumental gate on the West Berlin side with the crowning statue of Victory driving a chariot and four horses toward East Berlin, symbolically depressing for Westerners. In front of us on the Wall a sign warned: *ACHTUNG! SIE VERLASSEN JETZT WEST-BERLIN.* Warning! You are now leaving West Berlin.

We stood on the very spot where President Kennedy in 1963 had given one of his most famous speeches expressing solidarity with West Berliners, a free and democratic island within the communist GDR. He endeared himself to the free German people by declaring in German, "*Ich bin ein Berliner.*" I am a Berliner. During the Berlin Airlift, all Americans had been Berliners.

In the dark the high beam of the search lights pierced the inky black of no man's land surrounding the Gate to illuminate any defectors. But beyond the guard towers, lay East Berlin, eerily unlit, hunkered down beyond the lights like a giant beast retreating from a campfire to lurk menacingly in the underbrush. You knew it was there even if you couldn't see it. No lights for the East Berliners, but abundant light to expose any potential defectors at the Wall!

What a shock to our system when we returned to the Ku'damm emerging from the subway into virtual daylight created by the pulsing neon lights enticing us to eat or drink or dance. We ambled along, hand in hand, listening to the music that escaped from any open door, reading the menus posted outside restaurants, delighted with the seemingly endless choices. Yet, we couldn't escape the memories of small white crosses and anti-tank emplacements. We had already gained an appreciation for the frenetic activity in West Berlin. Everyone craved distraction. Everyone needed to forget, at least for a while, to take a mental holiday from the depressing reality of a divided city separated by a Wall.

The next morning, I was busy with my sewing kit ripping John's Spec 4 badge from his uniform sleeve. However, I could not get rid of the clearly darker, unfaded fabric that remained in the exact shape of the removed badge. Any idiot could tell a Spec 4 badge had been on that sleeve, but we could do nothing about it. He dressed and left to meet his tour of East Berlin. I had planned to window shop the Ku-damm, perhaps splurge on a last slice of black forest cake since I was leaving soon, but I found myself nervously pacing our room unable to do anything but worry.

I remembered my own day tour of East Berlin. Just as I had, John would enter through the American gate at Checkpoint Charlie. It was a simple-looking wooden guard shack, never embellished, because the US regarded a divided Berlin and the Wall as a temporary situation. Building a permanent structure would have said otherwise. I knew the East Germans would search under the bus with mirrors to see if any poor soul were clinging to the undercarriage. I knew they would open all of the luggage compartments and look under every seat. I knew they would poke a long wire into the gas tank. I knew that two steely-eyed, rifle-toting East German guards would board the bus and spend several minutes searching each face, comparing it with the picture in the passport, or on the ID in John's case, peering back and forth and back and forth until they were convinced that the person in front of them beyond all doubt matched the person pictured on the document. I remember how nervous I was having long hair in my passport photo, piled on top of my head, instead of the short, curly style I sported on my summer trip to Europe. Of course, for John, the possibility of being determined a spy upped the stakes.

At the end of the day, John found me trying to read in the hotel sitting room. Looking downcast and shaking his head, he started, "I can't believe it, any of it. There's no traffic, all those wide streets with no vehicles. And the piles of rubble, the walls of bombed-out buildings still standing, empty shells. It's like the war ended last year, not 25 years ago. And the smell . . . they only have coal briquettes for heat. We were all coughing." That was something I hadn't experienced having visited in the summer.

"And stores? Where do they buy anything, even groceries? I don't think I saw a single restaurant," he ranted, "but I sure saw a lot of East German Polizei . . . no shortage of those. Grim." Shaking his head, he crumpled into the deep chair next to mine. "Whadda' way to live . . . if you can call it that! Geez, it's bad enough to live in West Berlin with that depressing wall, but living behind it is not living at all," he sighed. He took my hand, solemnly staring straight ahead, "Man, how did we get so lucky being born in America?"

On our last day in Berlin we again strolled down the Ku-damm, this time until it turned into Tauentzienstrasse where we discovered the bombed remains of a ruined church spire sandwiched between two ultra-modern buildings, one a large, squat octagon, the other a tall, narrow hexagon. Berliners had nicknamed them the powder box and the lipstick. The complex was the Kaiser

Wilhelm I Memorial Church. Both the modern buildings looked like glass honeycombs. The exteriors appeared gray to us reflecting the gloomy, overcast day, but once inside the powder box—wow! The glass honeycombs projected a deep blue light, a peaceful and calming effect, as if from, well, heaven, a heaven more heavenly than any ever imagined, even on the brightest of sunny days. Just as the grandeur of the medieval cathedrals of Europe had mesmerized us, this modern building, entirely different in concept, produced an equally emotional response. In awe we sank immediately into the first pew inside the door to absorb the otherworldly atmosphere of the place.

From the powder box we entered the ruins of the old stone spire. It remained from a Neo-Romanesque church completed in 1895 crowning Bismarck's grand Ku-damm thoroughfare. During World War II, on December 23, 1943, Allied bombing heavily damaged this Kaiser Wilhelm I Memorial Church, and in April of 1945, the heavy air raids aimed at ending the war nearly destroyed it entirely. The hollow core of its West spire, however, remained. When a new church was proposed after the war, Germans protested the demolition of the hollow tooth, as they called the tower ruin. So, it remains as a remembrance of the destruction of war and as a symbol of reconciliation.

To enter we simply walked through a space left where a wall had once stood. Inside, a nearly intact, larger-than-life ivory statue of Christ, miraculously salvaged from the altar of the demolished church, stood among the blackened ruins looking down on us, an eerie reminder that we humans, who pursue war, are flawed beings. That we have failed to "love one another" and failed "to do unto others as you would have them do unto you." Yet, we are forgiven and must seek reconciliation with our fellow beings to gain peace.

Next to the statue of Christ hung a metal cross, fashioned from three huge iron spikes. In amazement we read that they had come from the bombed church of Coventry in England. We had been there in May. In Coventry on November 14 of 1940, incendiary bombs dropped by the German Luftwaffe had destroyed a magnificent Cathedral with the third tallest spire in England. That spire, like the hollow tooth, survived plus a partial shell of outer walls. The British also chose to build a new modern-style church next to their ruins, preserving them as, this sounds familiar, a remembrance of the destruction of war and a symbol of reconciliation. Behind the altar of the destroyed building, the Coventry Provost had these words engraved: FATHER FORGIVE.

Thou shalt not kill.
—The Bible, Exodus 20:13

There's nothing so much like a German soldier in his trench than a French soldier in his. They are both poor sods and that's all there is to it.
—Marie-Paul Rimbault, quoted by John Ellis in *Eye Deep in Hell: Trench Warfare in World War I*

To kill one man is to be guilty of a capital crime, to kill ten men is to increase the guilt ten-fold, to kill a hundred men is to increase it a hundred-fold. This the rulers of the earth all recognize, and yet when it comes to the greatest crime—waging war on another state—they praise it! . . . If a man on seeing a little black were to say it is black, but on seeing a lot of black were to say it is white, it would be clear that such a man could not distinguish black and white. . . . So those who recognize a small crime as such, but do not recognize the wickedness of the greatest crime of all—the waging of war on another state—but actually praise it—cannot distinguish right and wrong.

—Stephen Pinker,
*The Better Angels of Our Nature:
Why Violence Has Declined* 2012

BOOK FOUR
◆━━━◆
UNIVERSITY OF IOWA AND BEYOND

30

◆——————◆

Blessing or Curse?

December 1970: During 1970 an estimated 60,000 soldiers experiment with drugs according to the US command. Also, there are over 200 incidents of fragging, in which soldiers attacked unpopular officers with fragmentation grenades.

December 31, 1970: The Paris Peace talks conclude a second year without progress. US troop levels in Vietnam reach 334,600 Americans, 6,173 die.

I left Germany on December 5, 1970. As my plane lifted off the tarmac in Frankfurt, I found myself wiping away the tears, not because I was leaving John at Christmas. That was temporary. We knew that a few days after Christmas we could not only celebrate the holiday together, but also celebrate being together permanently, a normal married couple. In fact, I cried because I was leaving our life in Germany. Had this experience been a blessing or a curse?

Perhaps John's service as a Vietnam-era draftee became both a curse and a blessing in our lives. As an experience, it may not have been fatal, left no combat wounds, physically or mentally. The combat veterans who went to Nam risked wounds, maiming, and death. They came home with souvenirs, such as cancer from Agent

Orange and PTSD from the horrors they witnessed. War changes men.

In comparison to the sacrifices made by the real soldiers who fought in Vietnam, John's service feels paltry. How dare we whine about living in our garret apartment with the tilting bed; cleaning latrines; being stuck in a country where we didn't speak the language and couldn't watch television or use a telephone; living an ocean away from our families and facing a lost pregnancy without their support; delaying our education and professional life; or constantly fearing a transfer to Vietnam? We packed a lot of Carpe Diem into each and every day. In retrospect we both recognized our inconvenience to be minimal in comparison to those who served in Vietnam. However, being newly in love, the fear did shake us to our core. We felt cursed.

So, what were the blessings? I thought Germany had turned out to be the adventure of a lifetime. Little did I know that it would be the first adventure of a lifetime, as we eventually lived in Scotland, Australia, Papua New Guinea, and Kazakhstan. But more importantly, I now realize we grew up. I sensed that then. We became self-sufficient. We experienced life outside of Iowa and gained a wider perspective on our world. We thwarted obstacles, and, most importantly, we did it together. The experience bound us as a couple.

Eight hours after I had dried those parting tears in Frankfurt, the plane touched the tarmac at JFK. Again, I was in tears. The USA! The home of the free and the land of the brave! The country that had defeated Hitler! The country that must defeat Communism! The country of my birth, where my family lived. I was on US soil! I was home!

. . . the very problems you must overcome also support you and make you stronger in overcoming them.
> —George Pocock, quoted in
> Daniel James Brown's
> *The Boys in the Boat* 2013

What doesn't kill me makes me stronger.
> —Friederich Nietzsche,
> *Twilight of the Idols* 1888

I slept in my own room in my own bed in Bettendorf those first few nights enjoying all the pampering that my parents could bestow, especially my father's steaks on the grill and my mother's chocolate silk pie.

Then I borrowed Mom's car and drove to the farm near Newburg to see Vesta and William. I wasn't their John, but I was the next closest thing. I could talk about him, share first-hand his impressions of East Berlin, and lighten their loneliness just by being there.

On the way back, I stopped in Iowa City and stayed with the Kleins in their commune. It was great to see them, but I couldn't imagine going back to communal living. Four years in a dormitory and sorority house had been quite enough for me. I didn't want to negotiate chores with anyone else. John presented enough challenge in that department.

Besides my general discomfort with the situation, I don't remember getting any sleep as I had to crash on a lumpy, musty-smelling sofa in their unfinished basement. The house cat, who detected immediately that I was allergic to cats, spent the night pacing back and forth on the back of the sofa above me. With occasional breaks, she ran across my body to the drain in the slanted cement floor where she entertained herself by tipping the drain lid until she could spin it like a top. Eventually, it always plopped back into the drain reverberating through the darkness. Startled, she scampered back across my body to the top of the couch to pace again. Commune life was definitely not for me.

But in spite of the black bags under my eyes during the interview the next day, I landed a teaching position second semester in nearby Norway, Iowa, a town with no public or school libraries. However, they boasted about their lighted baseball field claiming Norway as the Baseball Capital of Iowa. At least I could relax and enjoy the Christmas season, trying to readjust to multi-colored Christmas lights that looked garish to me after the all-white or all-yellow German lights. A year before I had thought the German lights looked pale compared to the multi-colored lights of my childhood.

And I waited for John. My family decorated the tree as usual. I attended the Christmas Eve candlelight service with them, but on Christmas Day we listened to carols, played games, and read. For the presents and Christmas dinner, we all waited for John.

Finally, his call came the evening of the 28th. The army had flown him to Fort Dix in New Jersey that day. He was in the USA and hoped to be discharged the next day, but who knew how fast the army wheels might grind. The next call came in the early afternoon of the 29th. He was at the airport trying to fly military standby to Chicago O'Hare. Then he would connect to Moline, hopefully arriving in the evening on the last flight. But the next call came just as we finished dinner. The flight to Chicago had been delayed. They were finally ready to board now. He would be arriving too late to make the connection at O'Hare. He would have to sleep in the airport. It would be tomorrow before he could be home.

Dad was standing right there. He knew I was crushed, only one day, but . . .

He said, "Get your coat. We're going to Chicago."

I screamed and gave him an exuberant hug and kiss as I ran for my coat.

It wasn't until three hours later near the outskirts of Chicago that we realized we had no idea which flight John was on. It hadn't mattered on the phone when we thought he would connect the following day. So how would we find him? Since he didn't know we were coming, he wouldn't even be looking for us. We would have to page him and hope he heard. We parked and entered the terminal, and then a miracle happened. We looked up at the nearest escalator. There stood John gliding from above right toward us. I whooped. Dad yelled. John beamed. We all met at the foot of the escalator in a group hug. Indeed, it was a Christmas miracle in O'Hare Airport on December 29th, 1970.

We made it home after midnight where John got a huge embrace and even a kiss from his mother-in-law who was too excited to go to bed. He called his parents in spite of the hour, and then we crawled into bed together, a perfectly flat bed, back in the US of A. The next morning, we all opened Christmas presents around the tree. Most of them were from Germany, a Hofbräuhaus stein for John and another Hummel figurine for me, a school boy with a satchel of books on his back. Instead of being a surprise to the recipient, our presents were a surprise to the givers, Mom and Dad, who had sent me the money to do their shopping for them in Germany. Our main present that I had bought with their money was a curtained, German cradle in hopes that someday we would have babies to put in it.

John's parents arrived soon after we finished with the presents. Ever the stoic Scottish and Mennonite pioneers, they greeted him, after a year and a half, with a handshake, an economy of emotion. Not just William, but Vesta, too. Then we all sat down to Mom's traditional Christmas dinner featuring her standing rib roast. She knew how to sear the outside crisp and crunchy while holding the juices inside. Her rich gravy filled the house with its hearty aroma, the essence of comfort, home and family.

Every outbound soldier who moved through this place [Camp Atterbury] was traveling away from an ordinary life, and every inbound veteran returned to this same endless tract of yellow cinder block and brown shingles changed in ways they would only begin to recognize upon washing up against this familiar shore, no longer the same people they had been before.

—Helen Thorpe, *Soldier Girls* 2014

Who of you by worrying can add a single hour to his lifespan?

—The Bible, Matthew 6:27

Vietnam Becomes History: 1971-1989

June 13, 1971: The New York Times *publishes a series of front-page articles based on the Pentagon Papers, a top-secret Department of Defense study of U.S. political and military involvement in Vietnam. The documents show that the Kennedy Administration had helped with the assassination of South Vietnamese President Ngo Dinh Diem in 1963. Also, they reveal, contrary to public government statements, that the bombing of North Vietnam has made no impact on the North's will to fight.*

June 18, 1971: The U.S. Department of Justice obtains a temporary restraining order against further publication by the Times *on grounds that it is detrimental to U.S. national security.* The Washington Post, *having also obtained the papers, begins to publish them.*

June 30, 1971: In the case of New York Times Co v United States, *the US Supreme Court rules 6-3 that publication of the Pentagon Papers is justified as freedom of the press under the First Amendment because the papers pose no threat to national security.*

March 24, 1972: The film version of Mario Puzo's The Godfather *is released.*

November 7, 1972: The country reelects President Nixon despite the ongoing Watergate investigation.

November 21, 1972: On appeal all charges are reversed against the Chicago 7. The Justice Department decides against retrying the defendants.

January 27, 1973: All parties to the Vietnam Conflict sign a peace agreement in which a ceasefire is declared. The US agrees to withdraw combat troops.

March 29, 1973: The Vietnam Conflict officially ends for the United States. Military advisors and some Marines remain in-country, but the last US combat soldiers leave Vietnam. Of the more than 3,000,000 Americans who served in the war, almost 58,000 have died, over 1,000 are still missing-in-action, and 150,000 have been seriously wounded.

1974: The North Vietnamese break the cease fire and triumph in a series of battles advancing toward Saigon.

August 9, 1974: Due to the Watergate scandal, President Nixon resigns to avoid impeachment; Vice President Gerald Ford becomes president.

April 29, 1975: As Saigon falls to the North Vietnamese, a massive airlift ferries over 1,000 American civilians and 7,000 Vietnamese refugees to US aircraft carriers waiting offshore.

April 30, 1975: The North Vietnamese take Saigon; the war in Vietnam ends.

May 12, 1975: Time *magazine features Ho Chi Minh on its cover with this caption: "The Victor."*

April 13, 1982: The Vietnam Veterans Memorial, designed by American architect Maya Lin, opens adjacent to the National Mall in Washington, DC. It lists the names of all those killed or missing-in-action during the conflict in Southeast Asia inscribed on a black granite wall.

1989: Mario Puzo admits the influence of the Kennedy family in creating the characters of the Corleones in his novel The Godfather.

Epilogue 1

◆————◆

Glorify or Horrify?

1990s: Trade and diplomatic relations gradually resume between Vietnam and the US.

April 16, 1995: Robert S McNamara, Secretary of State to Presidents Kennedy and Johnson during the escalation of the Vietnam Conflict, releases a book titled In Retrospect: The Tragedy and Lessons of Vietnam. *The New York Times review of the book states that McNamara "offers the public a glimpse of his aching conscience."*

1996: The Library of Congress designates the film M*A*S*H *for preservation as part of its National Film Registry which includes films considered "culturally, historically, or aesthetically significant."*

1997: The American Film Institute issues its first list of the 100 Greatest American Movies of All Time including M*A*S*H *at number 56 and* Easy Rider *at number 88.*

1998: The Library of Congress designates Easy Rider *for preservation as part of its National Film Registry.*

December 1991: John and I ask our sons, Ryan and Evan, both freshmen, one at university and one in high school, where in the world do they want to go bad enough that they will go with us? My mom died in October, and John's dad passed away on December 15th leaving John and I as the oldest generation. Suddenly there would be no more Christmases with grandparents. Although our Christmases had always included the traditional tree and gifts, they represented the celebration of a birth to a family in Bethlehem, a metaphor for the joy of every family welcoming a new life, a celebration of the love for each other, the love of family being the ultimate gift.

Now, with such fresh wounds, how can we find the joy to celebrate? Hence, we ask the boys for a travel idea, a different way to celebrate. They consult briefly, for once agreeing on something. Raised with our German scrapbook on the coffee table and the beer steins and wine glasses displayed on the shelves by the fireplace, they want to go to Germany to see where John and I lived. And it doesn't hurt that they can ski the Alps.

Berlin and German reunification had been in the news frequently during the last two years since the Wall fell on November 9, 1989. Pieces of the wall, just chunks of concrete or corners of bricks, appeared for sale everywhere, even in Sky Harbor Airport in Phoenix when we visited my mother for what turned out to be her last Christmas in 1990. Both John and I want to experience a unified Berlin and Germany. That would be something worth celebrating.

Hurriedly, I book airline tickets. No one else wants to fly on Christmas Day, so it's wide-open and not too expensive. I buy guidebooks, the updated versions of our old friends the *Michelin Green Guide* and *Frommers Europe on $5 a Day,* but now it's *Europe on $25 a Day.* Then I try to find a guidebook that includes information on East Germany, now that it is open to visitors and tourism. We will drive from the airport in Frankfurt through former East Germany to Berlin. The Tattered Cover, the iconic book store in Denver, claims they have one due to arrive any day, so I am checking back frequently. John has to work until noon on Christmas Eve, and The Tattered Cover is only open until one o'clock in the afternoon. That morning I call one last time. The book, indeed, has arrived, so John comes home by way of The Tattered Cover with the only guidebook in Denver that covers former East Germany: *Guide to East Germany*, updated printing 1991.

So, for the first time ever, we exchange our gifts, just the four of us, on Christmas Eve, and on Christmas Day we fly to Frankfurt arriving the morning of the 26th. At the airport we rent a car. All of my big strong men pull a total collapse induced by jet lag, so I drive all day to Berlin. It is very quiet in the car. As darkness settles we reach the outskirts of the city. John takes over once we leave the autobahn, and I navigate. Without time for making any reservations before we left, we had chosen a likely sounding hotel from our *Frommers*, in the heart of the city, but off the main streets, less expensive and more authentically German. We have no idea if they will have vacancies. Looking for the address in the dark, we drive around and around on the one-way streets, back past the address given in the guidebook several times, before we decide where it has to be. Then we drive around the circuit a few more times looking for a place to park. Finally, I conclude I will just have to get out on foot.

"But Mom, it's dark. There's no sign. How can this be a hotel?" Ryan objects, thinking he is being the voice of obvious reason.

"How will we find you again?" Evan piles on showing his discomfort.

I feel loved, rare for the mother of teenagers.

John calls after me, "Don't forget to find out where I can park this thing!"

Where I figure the hotel should be, I proceed up the stone steps feeling under my feet the worn depressions from at least a couple hundred years of footsteps, and I try the front door, a heavy, wooden-paneled affair, almost two stories tall, with worn brass hardware. Sure enough, it doesn't budge. Locked tight. I feel along the wall near the door handle for a bell. Bingo! I push, holding it down, but can't hear anything from within. Then it comes, the answering buzz that unlocks the door. I scramble to enter before it stops buzzing. Inside it is just as dark as outside, but I take a step carefully sliding my foot across the floor in case of more stairs. As my body moves forward, yeah, the motion detector turns on the lights. In front of me, in between various office entrances, stands a grand stone staircase with balustraded railings and a discreet brass plaque announcing Hotel Pension Goethe. I climb to the landing where it turns and continues upward to the next floor a good 16-20 feet above. At the top a glass wall closes the staircase from the interior, but on the glass in gold baroque lettering, it confirms Hotel Pension Goethe.

A clerk behind the reception desk just inside sees me. Again, a buzz. I open this door and step into a pleasant sitting room with ornate curlicues of sculpted vines ringing the high ceiling characteristic of a bygone era. The trail worn in the faded carpet, once plush and cushiony underfoot, invites the weary traveler to take a seat in the somewhat shabby, over-stuffed chairs before the fireplace on this cold winter's eve. "Man, will they have vacancies this late in the day?" I worry. After cramming from a German phrasebook on the plane, I hope I can dredge up my old German phrases.

"*Guten Abend,*" I begin. That part comes easily and buys me time to think. "*Haben sie zwei Doppelzimmer frei?*" I manage to get out, but with a pause between each word.

"*Zwei?*" the clerk confirms.

"*Ja, bitte, zwei,*" I assure him sticking up two fingers.

Yes, we are in luck. I don't even look at the rooms. We need to be out of the car and traffic, and we need food! I return to the curb and wait and wait. I begin to think Evan might have had a point with his plaintive lament, "How will we find you?" But the car appears, I jump in, and we find the parking place in the dark, somehow.

I could feel the boys' apprehension as we walk from the parking lot to the hotel. After all, you don't have to look for a Holiday Inn in the dark. The boys don't understand that electricity can be a luxury. The system of buttons and buzzers further mystifies them. And when they discover the bathroom is down the hall, well, . . . it isn't a harmonious family moment.

We dump our suitcases and head for the closest restaurant. The menu in German becomes the next obstacle. They are starving, but what can they eat? No hamburgers, no peanut butter and jelly. We offer, if they can stand the wait, to find a McDonald's once we are done. Ryan spies the word R*umpsteak* on the menu and decides steak is just what he needs. In spite of our advice to choose the *Wiener Schnitzel* or the roast chicken, that the rumpsteak would not resemble the beef he knows in the

United States, he insists on having it his way. After all, what could his parents possibly know? We were probably just too cheap and didn't want to pay for a steak. Evan chose to wait for McDonald's. John and I order *Pomme frites*, French fries, with our meals and give them to the boys hoping to prevent their starvation.

Ryan's rumpsteak arrives. It is, indeed, like shoe leather, only enhanced with a vinegar-based sauce. He gags on his first bite, too tough to chew, too disgusting to swallow. Now he is ready for McDonald's, too. We offer him bites of our schnitzel and chicken. Being starved, he has to admit, grudgingly, that they are tasty.

For several days we make two stops for each meal, the first at McDonald's for the boys and the second at a German restaurant for John and me, but after tasting off our plates, eventually the boys don't want McDonald's any more than we do, especially at lunch when we can buy wurst and brotchen at the outdoor stands. And they discover the pastry shops with the black forest cake and chocolate rum balls. Life is good again. They begin to regard the hotel-in-the-dark as an adventure. The bathroom is always available when they need it and immaculately clean. The breakfast buffet includes home-made breads and rolls with cheese and cold-cuts. Hotel Pension Goethe exudes a gracious, if antique, ambiance and has survived two world wars. They start to imagine what might have happened within these walls or just outside.

The morning after the rumpsteak, we go in search of Checkpoint Charlie, or what remains of it. It's not in the guidebook, but then it isn't a cathedral, castle, or museum either. The late December rain doesn't stop us. It is typical for the time of year, tourists are not. Thank God for Goretex! We bundle up, hoods drawn tight around our faces, with only glasses and noses peeking out, a whole family of "four eyes." We don't get far before we have to duck into a shop to wipe our glasses so we can see our map and the street signs. I remember us having to do that over and over. The shops also provide a few moments of warmth, and we linger longer and longer as the damp cold seeps into our bones.

Eventually we find our way to the intersection of Friederichstrasse and Zimmerstrasse, the site of the former Checkpoint Charlie. But we can't find it! Our *Michelin Green Guide* says, "On Friederichstrasse is the famous Allied checkpoint where foreign motorists are obliged to pass to enter East Berlin." We may be challenged with our spotty glasses, but walking around and around the area, we see a tiny merry-go-round and ferris wheel as well as circular airplane and boat rides for small children. None are operating in the rain, but how different from the scary Checkpoint, the ultimate symbol of the Cold War. In the early days of the Wall in 1961, 36 Russian tanks had faced off against 10 US tanks at Checkpoint Charlie. Also, it had been the scene of daring escape attempts, some successful and some not. In 1962 an East Berlin teen had bled to death from wounds inflicted by East German guards in the barbed wire at the Checkpoint just steps inside the Eastern sector. Now it holds a children's amusement park. Checkpoint Charlie is gone!

Inquiring in one of our shop stops, we are directed to the Checkpoint Charlie Museum around the corner. In the museum we find out that the United States officially closed Checkpoint Charlie with military pomp in June 1990, a year and a half previously. How did we miss that? At the proceedings US Secretary of State James Baker said, "For 29 years Checkpoint Charlie embodied the cold war. We meet here today to dismantle it and to bury the conflict that created it." It, indeed, no longer exists. Through the years since, we have read that the metal shed in use when the wall fell became part of the open air Allied Museum in Berlin, and in 2003 a replica of the original wooden shack that we had passed beside in 1967 and 1970 respectively was set up as a memorial in its original location on Friederichstrasse. Now tourists can have their pictures taken in front of it with an actor dressed as a US military policeman!?!?! If we ever go again, we'll have to fish John's MP helmet out of the grandchildren's dress up box in the basement, so I can take a selfie with my real military policeman in front of Checkpoint Charlie!

After Berlin we travel through the former East Germany to Eisenach and visit Wartburg Castle where Martin Luther hid from Pope Leo X in 1521 after refusing to deny his beliefs at the Diet of Worms. To pass his time he translated the New Testament from Latin into German. We head for Mannheim and find Turley Barracks, but our map doesn't include the suburb of Feudenheim where we lived. I tell John that I think I can drive there if I set my brain to autopilot and let instinct guide me. I take over at the wheel and 10 minutes later we sit in front of 102 Arndtstrasse, Mannheim-Feudenheim.

Twenty-one years since we left, it has had a face lift with new shutters, refurbished and repainted stucco, and a new wrought iron fence and gate replacing the rickety wooden ones. Frau Schaeffer's rose jungle no longer droops over the sidewalk to the front door. A car is parked out front, so the boys have great fun positioning John for a picture in front of it with the house in the background. It must have the same angle as the picture they know so well from the scrapbook showing him in full MP regalia standing in front of our first car, the Opel, ready for work. From there we share the historic sites at Heidelberg and Worms with the boys and stay several days in Rothenburg ob der Tauber, reminiscing about our time there with their grandparents.

In Bavaria John and the boys ski the Zugspitze although conditions are icy and John mainly slides down on his backside. He must hang in there with his sons to guide the way. Skiing in the Alps is not like skiing in purpose-built US ski areas. You're not out in a national forest; you're in civilization, farms and villages, private property. You ski through people's yards and even gates, trying to avoid unfenced cliffs, past roads and over railroad tracks. The boys need Dad to read the signs, such as *verboten,* forbidden, or *gesperrt,* closed. Throughout the trip, we have encouraged them to go off on their own, not to feel tied at the hip to their old fuddy-duddy parents, the know-nothings, but they have stuck with us intimidated by the language, the currency, and the winding medieval streets that change name every other block.

We now spend hours at dinner, lingering over the great German food, talking over our adventures of the day, and plotting our adventures for tomorrow. Ryan is old enough to drink in Germany and enjoys feeling like an adult having a beer with his dad. We notice that another American family, one with daughters, is staying at the same hotel. They are noticeable because they quarrel constantly and loudly.

One morning after breakfast, when the boys have gone back to the room, the girls' mother stops at our table. "I've noticed what a good time your family is having," she says. "We're spending all of this money on this trip, but it seems our girls can't stand anything about this country. Mind if I ask what you're doing to keep your sons so happy?" This isn't a joke. She's not laughing. She wants to know. We give her the Frau Schaeffer shrug and roll our eyes. We don't know what to say. Indeed, the boys are enjoying themselves. Not only that, we realize they are enjoying our company. Germany has wrought a family metamorphosis: we are no longer the "stupid" parents, but have suddenly become not only wise, but even fun to be with.

1994-99: I am team-teaching American Studies in Jefferson County, Colorado. I organize my teaching of 20th century literature by spending a quarter on the decades, the 20s, 30s, 50s, 60s and 70s, and a quarter on World War I, World War II, and Vietnam in a unit I name "Literature of Conflict: Glorify versus Horrify." I grab the students right away by having a guest speaker, a former Green Beret, whose therapist has advised him to speak about his experiences in Vietnam. Allan Martin is brutally honest and encourages students to ask whatever they want. The questions run the gamut as some students are from homes where their father served but never talks about it, some from homes where their father served and is vociferously patriotic, and some are the offspring of protestors, draftees, or conscientious objectors. It's a public school.

Over a period of years, I hear Martin's story, some parts a repeat, but always something new and startling. His platoon, all Green Berets, was sent across the Vietnamese border into Laos following reports of the location of a Prisoner of War camp there. Supposedly, neutral Laos was off-limits for foreign troops; however, the North Vietnamese often slipped into the jungles just across the border with impunity. Martin's platoon knew if caught, that no officials back home would ever admit they existed. They were on their own. Indeed, they located the POW camp, deserted, but with warm tea left in the cups and warm coals left in the braziers. Who knew they were coming? Where had the Cong gone? Even though they couldn't have gone far, the Green Berets never found anyone. It came time for their rendezvous with a chopper that would extract them and return them to Vietnam. As they approached the designated clearing, the Cong ambushed them. Only Martin and one other soldier survived, and that soldier was wounded. Martin, staying alive by using survival techniques like eating maggots, carried his buddy back to Vietnam. The trickiest part, he always said, was getting back across friendly lines after two weeks in the rainforest as the two of them were filthy, barefoot, bearded, ragged, and unrecognizable as US soldiers.

The next day he was debriefed in the morning. His hitch had expired during the two week walk back, so by the end of the day, he boarded a plane in his dress uniform headed home. During the flight he kept replaying the events in his head. Were there any POWs alive in that

266

camp and what happened to them? How could we have botched saving them? How did the Cong find out we were coming? How had we allowed the enemy to slip away? How did they know the rendezvous coordinates for our pickup? The unescapable conclusion: someone had given them away. Who?

Landing in San Francisco, trying to balance his joy at returning to the US with survivor's guilt, wondering why he was the one to come home alive, he walked down the concourse where protestors spotted his uniform and began heckling him. When one spit in his face, he cracked.

"I'm not proud of it, but I did the guy serious damage," he admits. Still ringing in his head: "who was it? who gave us away?"

Usually a student would ask what was the worst thing that he faced.

The answer was always the same: "While attacking a Cong village, I killed a little girl. She kept walking toward me. I spoke Vietnamese. Several times I yelled, 'Stop!' But she wouldn't stop." Since children were often booby-trapped with explosives, Martin had to shoot not only for his own safety, but also for the protection of other soldiers around him.

Martin's sincerity and integrity win over my students, regardless of whether they have been taught at home that the Vietnam Conflict was just or was unjust, whether their parents enlisted or protested, whether hawks or doves. No one can imagine him being heckled or booed for his service. We all empathize and respect him.

Now my students conduct their own interviews with a combat veteran, either someone they know, often a father, uncle, or grandfather, or someone registered with a veterans' organization. They write oral histories, and always, the most amazing stories surface.

Joy always knew that her grandfather who ran an import/export business had a Japanese friend and partner who stayed with their family when he came to Denver on business. What she didn't know before this assignment was how they met: during World War II, her grandfather and his best friend from childhood became pilots together and were sent to the same squadron in the South Pacific. Grandfather watched a Japanese plane shoot down his buddy, who went down with his plane. Grandfather succeeded in shooting down the Japanese plane responsible before being shot down himself. He deployed his parachute and landed safely in the ocean. He was able to swim to the wreckage of his friend's plane bobbing in the ocean and found him dead in the cockpit. Then he spotted the Japanese pilot, who also parachuted, struggling in the water, the pilot who had just shot down his life-long best friend, the pilot he himself had shot down in revenge. Grandfather made his way to the struggling man and found that he was wounded. He saved the Japanese pilot who after the war became his friend and business partner.

Here's another oral history forever seared in my memory! Rick decided to interview his Korean War vet father, an American man much older than his Chinese mother. The family had recently relocated to our area from Singapore due to the father's retirement.

Rick's father said to him: "Son, perhaps this is a good opportunity to tell you about something, something I've needed to talk to you about, well, really, ever since I retired last year. Somehow, I didn't know how to begin, where to start. It's this: I never really worked for the "XYZ" company in Singapore, where you thought I worked. Actually, I worked for the CIA. I was a CIA operative."

Rick's oral history told about his father's first operation toward the end of World War II in Germany behind enemy lines. The Allies had discovered a printing operation, counterfeit printing of US dollars, which the Germans intended to dump on the international market in order to deflate US currency. The presses were set up in a barn and worked nearly around the clock except for a couple of hours after midnight. The Germans heavily guarded the dirt road into the isolated location, but only a single guard stood at the door to the barn during those two hours. Traveling to the barn on foot across open country, fields and forest, not on the road, Rick's father arrived at the barn at the exactly designated time and silently slit the guard's throat. That was his single piece of the operation. For security reasons none of the operatives knew each other or the details of the full plan. They completed their task at the designated time, alone, and left. As he made his way across a field on foot running for the cover of trees, he heard explosives and glanced over his shoulder only long enough to glimpse the barn being engulfed in flames. The explosion had been someone else's job.

Meanwhile, in class my students take a personal survey to start some soul-searching about their own beliefs and attitudes toward war. Then they start to list all the questions they can't understand about soldiers fighting in war.

It begins gingerly with one brave kid: "How can a man who has been taught all his life 'Thou shalt not kill' even become a soldier?"

Then a few more speak up.

"How can a soldier exposed to the atrocities of battle keep his sanity?"

"How do soldiers deal with knowing they face death constantly?"

And then they unburden.

"Do soldiers feel guilt and how does it affect them?"

"How do soldiers develop courage?"

"What makes a soldier a hero?"

"What affect does being a combat soldier have on the rest of a man's life?"

"Is war inevitable?"

I can't write on the board fast enough. They choose the question that bothers them the most and search for answers by reading their choice of short stories, nonfiction articles, poems, and a novel, all set during either World War I, World War II, or the Vietnam Conflict, their choice. Finally, they write personal essays grappling with their question and the insight they have gained through the literature and their oral history interview.

He said we were all cooked but we were all right as long as we did not know it. We were all cooked. The thing was not to recognize it. The last country to realize they were cooked would win the war.

—Ernest Hemingway,
A Farewell to Arms 1929

It was a movie about American bombers in World War II and the gallant men who flew them. Seen backwards by Billy, the story went like this: American planes, full of holes and wounded men and corpses took off backwards from an airfield in England. Over France, a few German fighter planes flew at them backwards, sucked bullets and shell fragments from some of the planes and crewmen. They did the same for wrecked American bombers on the ground, and those planes flew up backwards to join the formation.

The formation flew backwards over a German city that was in flames. The bombers opened their bomb bay doors, exerted a miraculous magnetism which shrunk the fires, gathered them into cylindrical steel containers, and lifted the containers into the bellies of the planes. The containers were stored neatly in racks. The Germans below had miraculous devices of their own, which were long steel tubes. They used them to suck more fragments from the crewmen and planes. But there were still a few wounded Americans though and some of the bombers were in bad repair. Over France though, German fighters came up again, made everything and everybody as good as new.

When the bombers got back to their base, the steel cylinders were taken from the racks and shipped back to the United States of America, where factories were operating night and day, dismantling the cylinders, separating the dangerous contents into minerals. Touchingly, it was mainly women who did this work. The minerals were then shipped to specialists in remote areas. It was their business to put them into the ground, to hide them cleverly, so they would never hurt anybody ever again.

—Kurt Vonnegut,
Slaughterhouse Five 1969

1995: While researching for resources to use in the Literature of Conflict unit, I stumble across this quotation from Civil War General and Senator Carl Schurz: "My country right or wrong." But it doesn't stop there! That part, usurped by the hawks for a bumper sticker during Vietnam, is only the beginning. It is out of context! Schurz continued, "When right, to keep her right; when wrong, to set her right." It is an aha moment for the teacher.

The role of the military and the role of the citizen need to be understood as separate and different. For military personnel they must follow the chain of command and obey orders. We need them to protect us, and we need to honor them for that. They need to be respected for their dedication to duty and bravery under fire. Their sacrifices should never be mocked or defiled as they were in the wake of Vietnam. If we disagree, it is with the Commander-in-Chief and Congress, who we argue with using our First Amendment rights and our vote.

Unlike soldiers, following orders is not the role of citizens in a democracy. Quite the opposite. Citizens must watch and reflect on the actions of their leaders. Their duty is "When right to keep her right; when wrong, to set her right." All citizens must feel the freedom and responsibility to question, to approach their government with skepticism, to debate without being branded as unpatriotic. That's what democracy means. Indeed, civil strife in the country during the Vietnam era eventually forced President Nixon to withdraw troops and conclude the war.

This year Robert S McNamara, the Secretary of Defense who advised both Presidents Kennedy and Johnson to escalate the Vietnam Conflict, publishes *In Retrospect,* an apology for his involvement. He quotes the Greek playwright Aeschylus: "The reward of suffering is experience," often translated from the Greek as "Wisdom comes through suffering." Over 58,000 young Americans *suffered* death for their leaders and descendants to gain this *wisdom.* We best honor them by remembering that lesson and refusing to put our troops in harm's way without just and adequate cause. They follow orders, but citizens in a democracy *keep her right* or *set her right.* We citizens should be able to say: "Hey, military men and women, we got your backs."

Michelle had a million doubts about the war in Iraq. Yet nobody else around her seemed to question what was taking place. . . . Because the other students felt at no risk of being drafted, the remote conflicts did not touch them personally. . . . It was war without the debate that had always accompanied war; war when only the poor had to serve.

—Helen Thorpe,
Soldier Girls 2014

Epilogue 2

◆———◆

In Flanders Fields

2002: The songs "Where Have All the Flowers Gone?" by Pete Seeger and "Alice's Restaurant Massacree" by Arlo Guthrie are inducted into the Grammy Hall of Fame honoring recordings of "qualitative or historical significance."

April 29, 2008: The number of American deaths as a result of the Vietnam Conflict reaches 58,220, and the government curtails record keeping.

2009: A Tony Award-winning revival of Hair opens on Broadway and subsequently tours the US including the Kennedy Center in Washington, DC.

October 2010: John and I have third-row aisle seats at the Kennedy Center for a revival of the rock musical *Hair*. No, we never did drugs, nor did we indulge in the sexual revolution. I don't even remember seeing the movie version of *Hair*. It didn't come out until 1979. By then we had two little boys and a mortgage. Yet, we loved the songs: "Hair," "Good Morning Starshine," and, of course, "Aquarius."

I will always remember the student who once asked me, "Mrs. Paul, you're an Aquarius, aren't you?"

"Aquarius? Why, yes. What makes you ask?"

"Just cuz you're the type of person who thinks all the animals in the woods are cute and fuzzy," he replied. After

275

some thought, I have embraced that sentiment. If I'm going to err in judging someone, particularly a student, I would rather err on the positive side until they bare their teeth. I firmly believe that fewer people react with a growl if you clearly expect a wagging tail.

So, we are in the audience and find the show not only opens all of the old issues about the Vietnam Conflict, but celebrates the era. Yes, not every war is a good war. Yes, kids need to know that. Yes, even though the draft no longer exists, we, as citizens, need to think for ourselves, not be sheep. The exuberance of the young actors and actresses make it feel as relevant as ever now with the Iraq, Afghanistan, and Syria conflicts grinding on.

At the end the cast involves the audience and brings any willing participants on stage to dance along with "Let the Sun Shine In." Much to John's horror, I stand up and climb the stairs to the stage. Feeling bound to protect me, from what I don't know, he follows along. So, we dance on the stage, forgetting the arthritis, the sciatica, John's cancer surgery scheduled next week, and we celebrate survival, our family, a lifetime together as we belt out the lyrics: "Let the sun shine in. Open up your heart and let it shine on in."

February 2013: We are on a tour of Vietnam, formerly our heart of darkness. During our trip the Vietnamese people, wanting our dollars, act friendly and hospitable, but at times the Communist government inserts their spin. Our visit today to the Cu Chi Tunnels, a vast network of hidden underground passages built during the war, is one of those times.

The guide encourages us to investigate one of the tunnel openings. A few people from the group disappear down a dirt hole that would have been concealed by branches. A few minutes later, they pop up unsuspected at various places nearby. Above their heads, they hold a small wooden-frame lid covered by sod matching the surrounding ground. None can fit through these tiny openings used by the Viet Cong, however, and so they replace the camouflaged lids and retrace their steps through the tunnel to where they entered.

These tunnels near Saigon connected to a system that underlaid much of the country. The Viet Cong spent their days in the tunnels and came out under cover of dark to surprise their enemy. Besides serving as living quarters, the tunnels held food and weapons caches, contained hospitals, and provided communication and supply routes. We are shown the camouflaged air vents, but are told that air quality was poor, food and water scarce, and insects, including poisonous centipedes and scorpions as well as vermin, infested the tunnels. Around half of the soldiers living there had malaria, and all had intestinal parasites which couldn't have improved the air quality. Yet they prevailed against the mighty United States and were proud of it.

Yes, they had support from their "brotherly comrades," the Chinese helping with artillery and engineering in the early years and the Soviets with radar systems and surface-to-air missiles later on. But the sandals on the ground were Vietnamese, their suffering undeniable while they fought on their own soil. While estimates of Vietnamese deaths during the conflict vary widely for many reasons, they fall between one and three million. They paid a high price and are proud of their victory and reunification. Yet, it pains us to see the defensive devices, such as the trap doors. When stepped on, they deposit the unsuspecting soldier into a pit of pointy-sharp, foot-long spikes. I know John is not enjoying "imagining himself living the life of an elector, wine glass in hand." Our hearts go out for those who faced this hell! We feared it and are so grateful that John never had to do it. Thank God!

> They [American colonial militia] did not fight us like a regular army, only like savages, behind trees and stone walls, and out of the woods and houses . . . [The colonists are] as bad as Indians . . . .
> —Anonymous British infantryman, following Battles of Lexington and Concord 1775

> Ca Mau, Vietnam>> Tam told [former Swift boat officer and Secretary of State John] Kerry the Viet Cong could hear the Swift boats coming from 3,000 feet away, and he gently suggested the lumbering Americans never stood a chance.
> "We were guerrillas," he said. "We were never where you were shooting."
> —Carol Morello, *The Washington Post* 2017

There is no instance of a nation benefitting from prolonged warfare. [T]he skillful leader subdues the enemy's troops without any fighting; he captures their cities without laying siege to them; he overthrows their kingdom without lengthy operations in the field." He also explained why this is: "When you engage in actual fighting, if victory is long in coming, then men's weapons will grow dull and their ardor will be damped."

—Sun Tzu, *The Art of War,*
sixth century BC

May 2014: We visit Durbuy, Belgium, not far from the German border, the same place that my mother's first cousin Richard Marchend, spelled with an *e* in the last syllable, was stationed briefly sixty years ago during the Battle of the Bulge. He was there in December. The Allies had recently seized from the Nazis the strategically important bridge in Durbuy, the cause of heavy fighting. Richard, given some free time after the fighting, strolled down the main road into the village enjoying an evening made peaceful by the fall of light snow. Glancing at the street sign, he realized he was on the Rue Henri Marchand, same last name as his except spelled with an *a* in the last syllable. Knowing his deceased grandfather Marchend emigrated to the US from the French part of Belgium, he wondered if the street might be named for one of his own ancestors. He knew that immigrants'

surnames often changed slightly due to clerical errors during the immigration process.

Richard approached a passerby and showed him his army dog tag pointing back and forth from his name to the street sign. The man registered his surprise and smiled broadly, then grasped Richard by the arm and led him up the street to the chateau, the only detached residence among the rows of connected townhouses forming the village. The man kept repeating, *"Bürgermeister, bürgermeister,"* the word for mayor.

At the chateau a small, middle-aged man opened the door. He was, indeed, Henri Marchand, the burgermeister and a Belgian *chevalier* or knight, as well as a direct descendant of the chap honored on the street sign hundreds of years previously. Henri welcomed Richard into his home, and, when Richard inquired about a possible family connection, Henri took him into his backyard to an aged headstone in the form of a cross, bearing a carving of the Marchand coat of arms in the center. Richard, who was his unit's photographer, had Henri take a picture of him with the coat of arms. It was in black and white. Richard, dressed in battle fatigues and helmet, knelt on one knee in the falling snow beside the stone. It's dark outside, and the contrasting white snowflakes dot the image. Alas, Richard was due back at headquarters and had to leave before they could talk further about family lineage. That picture, passed from generation to generation, became one of our family stories, in spite of the fact that no one knew if we were truly related to the aristocratic Durbuy Marchands, spelled with an *a*.

Now seventy years later genealogical research leads me to telephone the deceased Henri's son, Michel, a boy during the war, now in his late seventies. His telephone number is easy to find. Google shows a Michel Marchand living at No. 1, Rue Henri Marchand.

On the phone, in amazingly good English, he repeats my statement with a question mark, "You coming to Belgium?"

"Yes, we are coming to do genealogical research about my great-grandfather Marchend and his family in Liège."

"Liège close to Durbuy, very close. You come to lunch le chateau. We meet, must meet," Michel demands.

He knew all about the young American soldier named Marchend, who had appeared out of the snow on his family's doorstep back in 1944. The story of young Richard had become part of Michel's family history, too. On the night Richard arrived, the Nazis had just abandoned the chateau as their headquarters, and the family had come back briefly. Soon the Americans would move in.

A few weeks later, we arrive at the chateau for what turns out to be a seven-course luncheon. Michel, vigorous for his 79 years of age, proudly shows us his family home which he has been gradually restoring during his retirement, one gilded and wooden-paneled room at a time. The Nazis heavily damaged it during their stay in World War II, and he has lived most of his life in Brussels.

According to Michel, "They stole everything of value. But the Americans 'stole' only the white linen." After pausing to chuckle, he explains, "Actually, everyone in town collected and donated their white linens to the US soldiers, who made capes to use for camouflage in the snow." I know what he means. Before the trip I had googled Richard Marchend and found a photograph he had taken of a soldier in the snow wearing a white cape for camouflage.

Michel is an aristocrat used to being at the center of attention and enjoying it. He continues to tell his story. He believes the only reason he even has his ancestral home is due to the Americans. "It is quite amazing, these young men, most really only boys, came across the ocean, far from homes, far from families, to fight for Belgian freedom. So brave, brave in many ways. Many paid high price, too. We never repay them. No way to repay," he finishes, shaking his head and then looking down, head bowed.

Michel invites us to be his guests at a reception at the US Embassy in Brussels the next night. Meanwhile, during the day, I have had success searching for my ancestors in the government archives in Liège. Beyond any doubt, I realize we are not related to Michel at all. Indeed, our family has always spelled their name with an *e*, Marchend, even in the Old World. I am embarrassed about our imposition on Michel and about his hospitality, but then I think back to the ornate family tree on the wall of his library stretching back to the 1600s, each marriage decorated with the bride's coat of arms and the groom's coat of arms. Michel had to know all along that Richard could not be related, that we could not be related. I realize his hospitality has been about Belgian gratitude for my cousin's service and the service of all the young American soldiers in Belgium.

The US Embassy reception confirms my conclusion. The occasion: thanking Belgians who have helped

282

commemorate American military dead buried on Belgian soil. Michel Marchand is one such Belgian. He introduces us to many others. All express their thankfulness to us as Americans. They say that Americans have been true friends to Belgians. We have stood by their side. We have made their freedom and prosperity possible. We have our picture taken with the American Ambassador. The program for the evening is a slide-show presentation honoring Belgians for memorializing American dead buried in their country. With pomp and circumstance and lots of poppies they appear in images of ceremonies held at Henri-Chappelle, the Ardennes, and Flanders Field, all American World War I and World War II cemeteries in Belgium, all fields of white crosses stretching beyond the horizon. Two students take turns reading the famous World War I poem "In Flanders Fields," one in French and the other in English. I feel my stifled tears break loose sliding down my cheeks. In this moment, although I personally have done little to deserve it, I am proud to be an American.

In Flanders fields the poppies blow
Between the crosses, row on row,
That mark our place; and in the sky
The larks, still bravely singing, fly
Scarce heard amid the guns below.
We are the Dead. Short days ago
We lived, felt dawn, saw sunset glow,
Loved and were loved, and now we lie
In Flanders fields.
Take up our quarrel with the foe:
To you from failing hands we throw
The torch; be yours to hold it high.
If ye break faith with us who die
We shall not sleep, though poppies grow
In Flanders fields.
—John McCrae, "In Flanders Fields" 1915

Au champ d'honneur, les coquelicots
Sont parsemés de lot en lot
Auprès des croix; et dans l'espace
Les alouettes devenues lasses
Mêlent leurs chants sifflement Des obusiers.
Nous sommes morts,
Nous qui songions la veille encor'
À nos parents, à nos amis,
C'est nous qui reposons ici,
Au champ d'honneur.
À vous jeunes désabusés,
À vous de porter l'oriflamme
Et de garder au fond de l'âme
Le goût de vivre en liberté.
Acceptez le défi, sinon
Les coquelicots se faneront
Au champ d'honneur.
—French-Canadian Translation 191

Acknowledgements

I would like to acknowledge the help I received from Connie Shoemaker, Facilitator of the memoir-writing classes I took from the Osher Lifelong Learning Institute at the University of Denver, especially for introducing me to Bill Roorbach and his book *Writing Life Stories*.

I also appreciate my friends and response group members, the OLLI Writers, who evolved from Connie's classes. They helped me make what was clear to me clear to others.

A special thanks to David Gordon for reading this manuscript and commenting on all things German and in German.

And another thanks to Carolyn Kallemeyn, who helped resolve some thorny editing issues.

I also wish to recognize my brother Michael Vestle, who, in an early conversation about this project, characterized it as a "curse of interesting times."

Most especially I thank my husband, John, and my sons, Ryan and Evan, for sharing their comments and reactions, all of which contributed to my telling of this story.

Citations (Often Annotated)

This is a memoir, a work of creative nonfiction, not an academic paper. Therefore, I am not citing any information that can be easily located by entering key terms into a web browser. However, I do want to attribute quotations and a few esoteric facts and/or opinions to their sources. I avoid page numbers whenever possible as so many variations, including electronic editions and websites, make page numbers within the same text vary from one situation to another.

The cover picture of a female demonstrator offering a flower to a military policeman comes from the *National Archives*. It was taken at a Vietnam Conflict protest on October 21, 1967, in Washington, DC. Its access and use is unrestricted. See https://catalog.archives.gov/id/594360

In the Epigraph Senator Robert F Kennedy's speech was delivered on Affirmation Day at the University of South Africa. The News Release version appears twice in the Congressional Record and can also be found through the John F Kennedy Presidential Library.

In the Prologue the poem "A Decade" by Amy Lowell appears in her collection *Pictures of the Floating World* published in 1919. Today it is in the public domain and widely available on the internet. The quotation from Shakespeare appears in *Julius Caesar 2.2.1010–13*. The quotation from Antoine de Saint-Exupéry appears in his mostly autobiographic novel *Manon Ballerina* published posthumously in 2007. The table of Vietnam casualties appears in the *US National Archives*. It can be obtained online at www.archives.gov/research/military/vietnam-war/casualty-statistics.html#date

In Chapter 1 the Pete Seeger quotation from Plato's *Republic* was a favorite saying of Seeger's and appears in the *Smithsonian Magazine* article "Pete Seeger: Where Have All the Protest Songs Gone?" published April 2012 as well as in many other sources. The lyrics to "Where Have All the Flowers Gone" and information about their development come from the Folk Archives website at http://www.folkarchive.de/where.html The text of President Lyndon Johnson's televised address on March 31, 1968, can be found through the LBJ Presidential Library, the *NY Times*, and many other sources. The quotation from former Secretary of Defense Robert S McNamara comes from the Preface of his book *In Retrospect: The Tragedies and Lessons of Vietnam* published in 1995. The quotation from John Lennon's song "Beautiful Boy" written in 1980 for his son Sean appears in many places on the internet.

In Chapter 2 the quotation from Chimamanda Ngozi Adichie's novel *Americanah* appears in Chapter 4. The quotation from Jonathan Hull's WWI novel *Losing Julia* appears in Part I on page 48. The quotation from John Lennon and Paul McCartney's song "I Want to Hold Your Hand" appears in many places on the internet. Recorded by The Beatles in 1963, it became their first song to reach the top of the Billboard Top 100 in the United States. Professor Joshua Hook's quotation comes from an article titled "Here's what science says is the secret ingredient to making your love spark" by David Briggs in *The Washington Post* on February 12, 2016.

In Chapter 3 David O'Brien's testimony to the jury appears in Justice Earl Warren's opinion of the Court in United States v O'Brien handed down by the United States Supreme Court on May 27, 1968. The lyrics to Arlo Guthrie's "Alice's Restaurant Massacree" appear in numerous sources on the internet. The Declaration of Independence of the Democratic Republic of Vietnam appears in Ho Chi Minh's *Selected Works, Vol 3,* as well as many sources on the internet. The Mobilization chart comes from an article titled "Mobilization for the Vietnam

War: a Political and Military Catastrophe" by Col John Stuckey and Col Joseph Pistorius in *Parameters*, the journal of the US War College, published in 1985. The quotation from Dalton Trumbo appears in his horrific World War I novel *Johnny Got His Gun*. The lyrics to Pete Seeger's song "Turn, Turn, Turn," based on Ecclesiastes 3:1–2 from the Bible, appear in many sources on the internet. Yuval Noah Harari, Israeli historian and professor, makes this statement in his international bestseller *Sapiens: A Brief History of Humankind* in Part 2, the 6th chapter "Building Pyramids" under the heading True Believers.

In Chapter 4 historian John A Farrell's discovery of notes by HR Haldeman appears in a December 31, 2016, *New York Times* article.
In Chapter 5 the quotation from Dalton Trumbo appears in his novel *Johnny Got His Gun*. The quotation from Nelson Mandela appears in his autobiography *Long Walk to Freedom: The Autobiography of Nelson Mandela* copyrighted in 1995.

In Chapter 6 the quotation from Tim O'Brien's short story collection *The Things They Carried* appears in the story of the same title.

In Chapter 7 Sara Teasdale's poem "There Will Come Soft Rains" first appeared in her collection *Flame and Shadow* published in 1920, but it is now in the public domain and easily available on the internet.

In Chapter 8 the quotation regarding the infantrymen's rifle appears in Field Manual No. 23-8 issued by the headquarters of the Department of the Army in Washington, DC, on May 7, 1965. The quotation from Frank Pellegrini appears in a fourteen-part series published in *Time* magazine beginning November 5, 1999. It was written while Pellegrini attended US Army Reserve boot camp at Fort Jackson, South Carolina.

In Chapter 10 Neil Armstrong's quotation is common knowledge.

In Chapter 11 the quotation from Camus is often quoted by other authors so that even though the original source is out of print, this passage is easily found on the internet.

In Chapter 17 the quotations appear in my *Betty Crocker's New Picture Cookbook,* a wedding gift, published in 1961, in the "Meats" section under Poultry.

In Chapter 18 the remarks made by Senator Carl Schurz on the floor of the US Senate on February 29, 1872, appear in vol 45, p 1287, of *The Congressional Globe,* the publisher of Congressional debates from 1833-1873. The image of the Nazi party rally grounds in 1934 comes from the website Wikimedia Commons and is in the public domain. The original quotation from Voltaire in French appears in his book *Questions sur les Miracles* published in 1765. In English translation it appears in *Les Philosophes: The Philosophers of the Enlightenment and Modern Democracy* by Norman Lewis Torrey on pages 277-8 of that book.

In Chapter 19 the quotation from Idries Shah, the Sufi teacher and author, appears in his book *Reflections* in the section titled "Wasps."

In Chapter 21 the quotation from Anne Frank appears in the entry for July 15, 1944, of *The Diary of Anne Frank.* The letter from Otto Frank appears as breaking news on February 14–15, 2007, in numerous news sources in the United States, such as *The New York Times, The Washington Post,* and *Time* magazine. I also include part of the news analysis regarding the letter reported on February 14, 2007, by National Public Radio. The quotation from Viet Thanh Nguyen comes from *Nothing Ever Dies,* his nonfiction book on the Vietnam Conflict and memory, published in 2016. It appears in Chapter 3 "The Inhumanities."

In Chapter 22 the Lemony Snicket quotation appears in *Series of Unfortunate Events #3: A Wide Window*. The author's real name is Daniel Handler.

In Chapter 23 the lyrics to John Lennon and Paul McCartney's song "Revolution" recorded by the Beatles in 1968 appear in many places on the internet. The lyrics to "Ohio," written by Neil Young and recorded by Crosby, Stills, Nash & Young in 1970 appear in many sources on the internet. The quotation from Viet Thanh Nguyen's 2016 Pulitzer Prize-winning novel *The Sympathizer* about the Vietnam Conflict begins that book. The dialogue from the film *M*A*S*H* comes from the IMDb website. The quotation from Joseph Heller's World War II satirical novel *Catch 22* appears in Chapter 5 of that novel. The quotation from George RR Martin's novel *A Game of Thrones* appears in Chapter VIII of that novel.

In Chapter 24 the lyrics to John Lennon's song "Imagine" recorded solo in 1971 without the Beatles can be found in many places on the internet. The quotation from Rhett Butler spoken to Scarlet O'Hara in both the novel and film version of *Gone with the Wind* is common knowledge in the United States.

In Chapter 26 the quotation regarding Hitler's rise comes from a tourist booklet I purchased on the Obersalzburg in 1970. It credits Silvia Fabritius as the writer, Dale Shumanski as the translator, Verlag Silvia Fabritius as the publisher and the local daily newspaper, the *Berchtesgadener Anzeiger*, as the printer. It is undated. My version of Mad King Ludwig's death, although speculative, is based on recent evidence as reported on February 6, 2014, in *The Daily Telegraph* in London.

In Chapter 27 the lyrics to John Lennon's song "Give Peace a Chance," which he recorded with his wife Yoko Ono, appear in many sources on the internet.

In Chapter 29 President John F Kennedy's famous quotation is common knowledge in Germany. The quotation from Marie-Paul Rimbault appears in a book by John Ellis *Eye Deep in Hell: Trench Warfare in World War I* on page 169. The quotation from Stephen Pinker in his book *The Better Angels of Our Nature: Why Violence Has Declined* appears on page 104. The quotation from the Bible in Exodus 20:13 comes from the King James Version.

In Chapter 30 the timeline information about drug use and fragging appears on *The History Place* http://www.historyplace.com/unitedstates/vietnam/index-1969.html The quotation of George Pocock in Daniel James Brown's *The Boys in the Boat* appears in the Epigraph to Chapter 4. The quotation from Friederich Nietzsche's *Twilight of the Idols* appears in the section "Maxims and Arrows." The quotation from Helen Thorpe's *Soldier Girls* published in 2014 appears in Part I: Chapter 6 "The Tiki Lounge." The quotation from the Bible in Matthew 6:27 comes from the King James Version.

In Epilogue 1 the quotation from Secretary of State James Baker appears in the speech he gave in West Berlin on June 22, 1990, celebrating the removal of Checkpoint Charlie. It was widely reported in US newspapers, such as *The New York Times*. The quotation from Kurt Vonnegut's World War II novel *Slaughterhouse Five* appears in Chapter 4 of that book. The quotation from Ernest Hemingway's World War I novel *A Farewell to Arms* appears in Chapter 21. The Carl Schurz quotation is repeated from my Chapter 18. See citation there. The quotation of Aeschylus from Secretary of Defense Robert S McNamara appears in the Preface of his book *In Retrospect* published in 1995. The quotation from Helen Thorpe's *Soldier Girls* appears in Part I: Chapter 5 "High Altitude" published in 2014.

In Epilogue 2 the lyrics to the song "Let the Sun Shine In" from *Hair: The American Tribal Love-Rock Musical* appear in many places on the internet. The quotation from an anonymous British infantryman appears in a collection of British and American accounts of the Battles of Lexington and Concord on April 19, 1775, that was compiled by Vincent JR Kehoe and titled *We Were There*. Privately printed it is available at Minutemen National Park in Concord, Massachusetts. The quotation from 6th century BCE military general and strategist Sun Tzu's *The Art of War* appears in Chapter II: Waging War. Carol Morello's story reporting John Kerry's return to Vietnam appears in *The Washington Post* on January 14, 2017. The poem "The Poppies in Flanders Fields" by Canadian John McCrae first appeared in the London magazine *Punch* on December 8, 1915, and subsequently, as the title poem in a collection by McCrae *In Flanders Fields and Other Poems* published in 1919. Since the bilingual Canadian government often uses it in official ceremonies, an official French translation titled *Au champ d'honneur* exists. Now both versions of the poem are in the public domain widely available on the internet.

I also enjoyed perusing my old copies of our German guidebooks. The *Green Guide* to *Germany: West Germany and Berlin* was published in 1986, and the *Guide to East Germany* was published in the USA by Hunter Publishing with an updated printing in 1991. Those books, especially the *Green Guide*, as well as our scrapbook of personal photographs and memorabilia helped me with historic background and recollection of details used in descriptions of historic sites in Germany

From Our German Scrapbook

1969: John in front of 102 Arndtstrasse

1969: Pat in Heidelberg

1969: John ready for street patrol;
Pat on the banks of the Rhine River

1970: Mom with her purse and Dad with his pipe

1991: Ryan, Pat, and Evan at the
Brandenburg Gate in former East Berlin

About the Author

PATRICIA ANN PAUL's world view developed from living in West Germany, Scotland, Australia, Papua New Guinea, and Kazakhstan as well as traveling in 49 states and in over 50 countries. Most especially, she values the opportunity of teaching and learning from her students at the high school and university levels in former West Germany, Papua New Guinea, and Kazakhstan.

Now she is a retired educator having taught students from sixth grade to the master's level in the fields of literature, composition, and education. Training and participation in the National Writing Project has enhanced her professional life. She has shared her learning and research with high schools, school districts, and school boards. She is Past-President of the Colorado Language Arts Society presenting at CLAS conferences and publishing in their journal.

In retirement she enjoys teaching literature, history, and writing classes for the Osher Life-long Learning Institute at the University of Denver and has published in OLLI's literary magazine *Reflections*. In her spare time, she relaxes by traveling, walking in the pine trees in Colorado, attending her grandchildren's athletic events, and reading and discussing thought-provoking books.